D1527801

Plato was one of the greatest thinkers of all time. His voice is the most
eloquent in the choir of philosophy,
and his wisdom is as fresh and mean-
ingful today as it was in the Golden
Age.

Extracting the essence of Plato,
the authors have presented him to us
simply and lucidly. Their brilliant interpretation makes it possible for the
reader to grasp, as he never has before, the meaning of this supreme
philosopher.

THE WISDOM
AND IDEAS OF
PLATO

former title: THE GREAT IDEAS OF PLATO

by
Eugene Freeman
and
David Appel

A Fawcett Premier Book

FAWCETT PUBLICATIONS, INC., GREENWICH, CONN.
MEMBER OF AMERICAN BOOK PUBLISHERS COUNCIL, INC.

Published by Fawcett World Library,
67 West 44th Street, New York, New York 10036
Printed in the United States of America

For Annette and Marge

CONTENTS

Authors' Note

THE PURSUIT OF PHILOSOPHY can be provocative and exciting and of immense practical importance. The ideas of philosophy are catalytic agents, and in their presence the mind is activated and stimulated into creative, integrated thinking.

It is our conviction that the basic ideas of modern civilization are in their essence simple ideas even though their significance is inexhaustible. They are simple and clear enough so that even the lay reader can come to grips with them, provided they are presented not only in their historical context, but as living ideas which are applicable and significant in the world in which we live.

No one can present the ideas of the great philosophers as eloquently and persuasively as they do themselves in their own writings. For this book we have accordingly selected from the original sources some of Plato's principal ideas expressed in his own words. It is admittedly a hazardous undertaking to present rather brief quotations out of their original contexts, with the risk of loss of intelligibility and distortion of meaning. We have tried to minimize these risks by selecting for quotation particularly those passages in which the author presents a relatively self-contained unitary idea which is clear and reasonably complete when taken out of its context, and which is written in his own most readable style. We also deliberately have refrained from paraphrasing or simplifying any of the quoted citations, since one of our principal purposes is to demonstrate to the general reader that the classics of philosophy are written in a style that he can understand and enjoy, after he has learned how to read them and how to appreciate them.

Our own commentaries, which follow each of the citations from Plato, are not intended to serve as anything more than elementary demonstrations of how the reader himself can develop his abilities to read with critical, philosophical insight. The first step in the development of critical insight is to learn to read with appreciation. Ideas that are taken into the mind passively without producing any interaction with any other ideas in the mind, are neither understood nor appreciated. Instead, if they are stored away without any awareness of their significance, they are virtually buried alive.

Understanding and appreciation are very closely related. It is impossible to appreciate an idea which is not understood; on the other hand, it is virtually impossible not to appreciate an idea which is understood. Yet understanding and appreciation are not the same. To understand an idea is to know what it means; to appreciate an idea is to know its value. Thus to understand an idea is to know what it signifies; to appreciate an idea is to know its significance.

An advance is made in our understanding of the great ideas when we are able to translate them from the language and context of the original philosophies in which they were first presented into the more familiar language and context of the everyday world in which the modern reader lives. A corresponding advance is made in our appreciation of the great ideas when we are able to relate them to the problems which are of vital importance to us today, in the context of the culture in which we are now living. It is at this level of appreciation that we discover the ideas to be the living forces which have gradually and almost imperceptibly shaped our culture, and are continuing to do so with an irresistible compulsion.

A second advance in understanding and appreciation is made when the reader discovers the profound modifications which have been made in the great ideas by the successive philosophers who have made them their own and refashioned them. It has been said that philosophy never quite recovers from the shock of a great philosopher. It is an intellectual experience of the first magnitude for the reader to go to the philosophers in their historical chronological sequence, and to learn from them to understand and appreciate the life and growth of ideas. The great ideas endure; but each great philosopher finds a new significance in them, as he reshapes them into his own living system of ideas, in which the ideas of his predecessors have been absorbed and re-expressed in an original form and with a new role.

As the reader becomes aware of the fundamental oppositions as well as the fundamental agreements among the ideas of the philosophers who have been his teachers, he learns to take stock of the ideas which he himself has made his own—to weigh and test them, and to resolve the inconsistencies among them of which he was previously unaware. As he gains his critical awareness of the inconsistencies and limitations of his own growing philosophy, which he is continually modifying and revising, he reaches a third level in his ability to understand and appreciate the philosophical classics. He learns to evaluate the significance of the ideas he reads, through his awareness of the changes and modifications they compel him to make in his own personal philosophy.

This book is not offered as either a text book on, or a substitute for, the writings of Plato. Its purpose is to acquaint the general reader with some of the enduring ideas of our civilization, as presented in the writings of one of our greatest philosophers; to extend our friendly encouragement to him; to offer a helping hand as he learns how to read and how to appreciate philosophy. It is our hope that we can help to give him the zeal and the courage to go on from our own simple book to the original writings of Plato himself.

EUGENE FREEMAN

DAVID APPEL

Introduction

Plato was one of the greatest thinkers of all time.
Like his immortal tutor, Socrates, Plato was a lover of
wisdom, a crusader against error, and an enemy of false-
hood. No one who listens to his words can forsake
philosophy.

The voice of Plato is the most eloquent in the choir of
philosophy, if not in the whole realm of secular literature. For the young and eager mind there is no more
inspiring approach to the great ideas than to hear them
come to life as Plato speaks.

He was born about 427 B.C., the son of noble and
wealthy Athenian parents. At the age of twenty, he became a disciple of Socrates, the greatest intellect of his
day. The respect and admiration of student for teacher
was profound and lasting.

In the year 400 B.C., Socrates was executed on charges
of corrupting the Athenian youth. Plato, together with
other disciples of Socrates, then left Athens, and traveled

widely abroad in the ancient world of Egypt, Italy, and Sicily. Later Plato returned to Athens to establish his famous Academy, the first university in Europe, where he taught until he died at the age of eighty-one.

Among the Platonic writings, the *Dialogues,* of which about thirty-five have been preserved, are regarded as masterworks. They reflect a mind of great dignity; they show broad vision; they mirror a man who lived a score of centuries ahead of his times.

High moral views, rich yet delicate irony, and superb dramatic artistry are all combined in the *Dialogues.* The positive teachings of Plato, in which his lofty absolute idealism is the all-pervasive and dominant theme, are very rarely stated directly. Plato was one of the greatest literary artists who ever lived, and his style is the artistic counterpart of his philosophy. The ultimate ideals of Plato's philosophic vision are ineffable and inexpressible; and not even Plato himself could capture them directly in words. Instead, he half suggests them through the subtle and artistic devices of his matchless style, through which shimmering glimpses of the Platonic Forms, evanescent and ever-changing, are caught as in a moving mirror.

His style abounds in the rich symbolism of poetic prose, in metaphor, allegory, and myth, and most of all, in provocative dramatic conversations which were written to expose confused thinking and fallacious reasoning by demonstrating that they lead to absurdities. These conversations exhibited the characteristic art of the philosopher, called dialectic, the search for the Ideas "through words." Through the questions and answers of the dialectic, even when they terminate in apparently confused and contradictory results, the reader makes the disconcerting but most stimulating discovery that the ideas which we have in our minds, and the words which we use to express them, do not fit each other very well, and that if we wish to clarify our ideas, we must examine the consequences and implications of the words we use when we attempt to express our ideas.

It has been said that there is no problem of philosophy

about which the first word was not written by Plato; and there are many who believe that Plato had the last word as well. He taught that Ideas are alive, eternal and immutable. The great paradox which constitutes the core of Plato's central teaching is that true reality is to be found only in the world of Ideas, and that the world we live in is only an imperfect imitation of that real world.

The world we live in, Plato called the world of sights and sounds, because we know it through our senses. However, we can never discover eternal Ideas, or Forms, through the medium of our senses. Only through our minds, through our reason, can we find out what Ideas are. The world of our senses is a temporal world, changing, mutable; the world of Ideas is everlasting, unchanging, immutable.

Perhaps the best illustration of how Plato looked upon this world of Ideas can be drawn from geometry. You can draw a circle which is a crude approximation of the idea of circularity. But the idea of circularity, to whatever extent it can be known, we can apprehend through our minds alone. The circles that we draw with our instruments are not real circles, because they are not drawn with lines made up of points, which have no thickness and no breadth.

Any circle that we draw must have enough thickness, or breadth, or extension, to be visible. But if it is drawn with a line that is thick enough to be visible, then it is only an imitation of the "real" circle, which is an idea or concept without physical existence.

Nevertheless, it is the Idea of the circle, that is, the concept of circularity, which makes the crude figure which we are able to draw on paper suggest something of what is meant by the Idea of a circle.

Plato would have said that the circle on the paper reminds us of the idea which we knew in a previous existence—or he would have said that the circle which we see with our eyes (i.e., the empirical circle) "participates" in the reality of the true circle, or pure idea, or form, or pattern.

Plato's ideas participate in our every-day world, even

though they can never be fully or successfully realized there. A sculptor or a painter who looks at a work of art he has created is never satisfied. With his mind's eye he can see how the work of art before him, no matter how successfully executed, only approximates the Idea, without reaching it. For the scientist, however, as Plato saw it, this "independent reality" is the only true measure of knowledge.

Ideas, for Plato, are ideals which set the standard of perfection for the imperfect world which we know by means of our senses. The life of the philosopher consists in the worship of ideas. For Plato, the greatest Ideas were the Ideas of the True, the Good, and the Beautiful. Like the Trinity these three were one—Truth is good and beautiful; the Good is true and beautiful; and the Beautiful is true and good. The search for the Ideas, the appreciation of the Ideas, and the participation in the Ideas —these constitute the love of wisdom, which is philosophy. The life of the philosopher is therefore a life of goodness, of truth, and of beauty.

In the world in which we live, the philosopher can never find the complete expression of these immortal and eternal Ideas, but he is tireless in his quest for them; and his life is a sustained effort to live by these Ideas, and to teach others to do so.

Plato's philosophy is therefore a philosophy to live by —a philosophy for youth—a moral system that places the stress on values rather than on facts or on things. As such, it is an antidote for rampant materialism. It holds nothing for the jaded or the cynical, for the aged or the weary in spirit. It is in truth a philosophy that lifts the human spirit on wings of living words which are as vital and as pertinent today as that time, almost twenty-five hundred years ago, when they were first spoken and transcribed.

Why Socrates Was The Wisest Man in Greece

SOCRATES is on trial for his life. He is charged with worshiping strange gods and corrupting the youth. He is replying to his accusers by explaining how his whole life has been dedicated to the religious mission imposed upon him by the oracle at Delphi. His was the mission of philosophy—of searching for wisdom and exposing ignorance without compromise and without fear.

(From "The Apology")

SOCRATES *And here, O men of Athens, I must beg you not to interrupt me, even if I seem to say something extravagant. For the word which I will speak is not mine. I will refer you to a witness who is worthy of credit; that witness shall be the God of Delphi—he will tell you about my wisdom, if I have any, and of what sort it is. You must have known Chaerephon; he was early a friend of mine, and also a friend of yours. Well, Chaerephon, as you know, was very impetuous in all his doings, and he went to Delphi and boldly asked the oracle to tell him whether—as I was saying, I must beg you not to interrupt—he asked the oracle to tell him whether anyone was wiser than I was, and the Pythian prophetess answered, that there was no man wiser.*

Why do I mention this? Because I am going to ex-

plain to you why I have such an evil name. When I heard the answer, I said to myself, What can the god mean? and what is the interpretation of his riddle? for I know that I have no wisdom, small or great. What then can he mean when he says that I am the wisest of men? And yet he is a god, and cannot lie; that would be against his nature. After long consideration, I thought of a method of trying the question. I reflected that if I could only find a man wiser than myself, then I might go to the god with a refutation in my hand. I should say to him, 'Here is a man who is wiser than I am; but you said that I was the wisest.' Accordingly I went to one who had the reputation of wisdom, and observed him—his name I need not mention; he was a politician whom I selected for examination—and the result was as follows: When I began to talk with him, I could not help thinking that he was not really wise, although he was thought wise by many, and still wiser by himself; and thereupon I tried to explain to him that he thought himself wise, but was not really wise; and the consequence was that he hated me, and his enmity was shared by several who were present and heard me. So I left him, saying to myself, as I went away: Well, although I do not suppose that either of us knows anything really beautiful and good, I am better off than he is,—for he knows nothing, and thinks that he knows; I neither know nor think that I know. In this latter particular, then, I seem to have slightly the advantage of him. Then I went to another who had still higher pretensions to wisdom, and my conclusion was exactly the same. Whereupon I made another enemy of him, and of many others besides him.

Then I went to one man after another, being not unconscious of the enmity which I provoked, and I lamented and feared this: but necessity was laid upon me,—the word of God, I thought, ought to be considered first. And I said to myself, Go I must to all who appear to know, and find out the meaning of the oracle. And I swear to you, Athenians, by the dog I swear!—for I must tell you the truth—the result of my mission

WHY SOCRATES WAS THE WISEST MAN IN GREECE 19

was just this: I found that the men most in repute were all but the most foolish; and that others less esteemed were really wiser and better.

The word philosophy is derived from "philo," meaning lover of, and "sophia," wisdom. The love of wisdom, which is thus the essence of philosophy, is a way of living. It consists of the unremitting testing and probing and intensive examination of our beliefs and their logical consequences.

Many of the beliefs held by the social and political leaders in a society, whether that of ancient Athens or of our own, are frequently unable to stand in the light of critical scrutiny.

The immortal idea to which Socrates dedicated his life, and to which he sacrificed himself, is nowhere stated more eloquently than in the brief citation from the "Apology."

Socrates points out a truth we often forget—that the first step towards wisdom is the discovery and the acknowledgment of our own ignorance.

The method of Socrates is explosively effective as a "debunking" device. It convinces even the most arrogant and conceited know-it-all that in his previously held convictions he has not only been wrong, but ridiculous as well.

If the victim of a devastating Socratic deflation happens to be a prominent person, we can understand his mortification at not only seeing his cherished beliefs crumble around him, but at having irretrievably lost face. If the love of wisdom is not in him, he will never forgive the man who has punctured the conceits which he had cherished as truth.

It is easy for us to see how inevitable the martyrdom of Socrates was. The wounds that his victims had suffered at his hands had never healed, for a small-minded man never recovers from an injury to his ego and self-esteem.

The man who is a true disciple of Socrates, as countless thousands have been through the last twenty-five hundred years, is grateful to the teacher who makes him aware of his own ignorance. An old Eastern proverb says:

> "He who knows not, and knows not that he knows not, is a fool, shun him. But he who knows not, and knows that he knows not, is a wise man, follow him!"

There can be no doubt that Socrates was fully aware of the inevitable consequences of his role as the self-appointed debunker of Athens. He must have known that a day would come when the enemies he had made would bring about his death, but this did not deter him from philosophy, the love and pursuit of wisdom.

The Parable of The Gadfly

As HIS TRIAL CONTINUES, Socrates introduces into his defense the parable which epitomizes his life and mission. He speaks of himself as a gadfly appointed by God to sting and prod the sluggish steed, which is the State, out of its slumber and ignorance.

(From "The Apology")

SOCRATES *And now, Athenians, I am not going to argue for my own sake, as you may think, but for yours, that you may not sin against the God by condemning me, who am his gift to you. For if you kill me you will not easily find a successor to me, who, if I may use such a ludicrous figure of speech, am a sort of gadfly, given to the state by God; and the state is a great and noble steed who is tardy in his motions owing to his very size, and requires to be stirred into life. I am that gadfly which God has attached to the state, and all day long and in all places am always fastening upon you, arousing and persuading and reproaching you. You will not easily find another like me, and therefore I would advise you to spare me. I dare say that you may feel out of temper (like a person who is suddenly awakened from sleep), and you think that you might easily strike me dead as Anytus advises, and then you would sleep on for the remainder of your lives, unless God in his care of you sent you another gadfly. When I say that I am given to you by God, the proof of my mission is this:— if I had been like other men, I should not have neglected my own concerns or patiently seen the neglect of them during all these years, and have been doing yours, coming to you individually like a father or elder brother, exhorting you to regard virtue; such conduct, I say, would be unlike human nature. If I had gained anything, or if my exhortations had been paid, there would have*

21

been some sense in my doing so; but now, as you will perceive, not even the impudence of my accusers dares to say that I have ever exacted or sought pay of any one; of that they have no witness. And I have sufficient witness to the truth of what I say—my poverty.

Some one may wonder why I go about in private giving advice and busying myself with the concerns of others, but do not venture to come forward in public and advise the state. I will tell you why. You have heard me speak at sundry times and in divers places of an oracle or sign which comes to me, and is the divinity which Meletus ridicules in the indictment. This sign, which is a kind of voice, first began to come to me when I was a child; it always forbids but never commands me to do anything which I am going to do. This is what deters me from being a politician. And rightly, as I think. For I am certain, O men of Athens, that if I had engaged in politics, I should have perished long ago, and done no good either to you or to myself. And do not be offended at my telling you the truth: for the truth is, that no man who goes to war with you or any other multitude, honestly striving against the many lawless and unrighteous deeds which are done in a state, will save his life; he who will fight for the right, if he would live even for a brief space, must have a private station and not a public one.

The real issues which resulted in the trial of Socrates were never mentioned in the courtroom. Socrates was actually the most dangerous public enemy the political rulers who had seized control of the state ever had to face. He not only thought for himself, but he was teaching the youth of the state to think.

When the rulers of a state demand of their subjects a blind and unquestioning subservience of thought, they cannot tolerate the man who teaches others to think. He must be purged. The accusers of Socrates did not want him to die. He was too beloved a public idol, and to make a martyr of him was a risky last resort. But he had to be silenced.

THE PARABLE OF THE GADFLY 23

His accusers would have far preferred to have Socrates accept a lesser penalty, such as exile, which would have rid them of Socrates without running the risk of arousing public indignation and revolt. In the figure of the gadfly, Socrates could very well have been hinting to his accusers that the giant steed, when goaded out of its lethargy, could strike dead not only the gadfly which had awakened it from its slumbers, but the captors who had enslaved it as well. As we will see in the "Crito," even after Socrates was waiting in the death cell for the execution of his sentence, the doors of the prison were virtually left wide open for him so that he could escape from the country. It is highly improbable that these arrangements could have been made without the secret consent and approval the political leaders to whom Socrates, the free citizen of Athens, or Socrates, the martyr of Athens, was a dangerous menace.

The charges which were trumped up to make a case against Socrates were, ironically enough, inspired by his genuine religious fervor and devotion. Socrates believed in God, with a sincerity and a depth of faith that few men have ever surpassed. The "strange gods" which Socrates was charged with worshiping were not gods or demons at all. As every reader of Plato knows, the admonitions which were heard and obeyed by Socrates were spoken to him by an inner voice, the voice of his religious conscience.

This was the voice which would never permit him to continue in an action which was wrong, or even to engage in one. He worshiped this voice as the voice of God. It could have been. Few men have ever known a better guide.

The Unexamined Life Is Not Worth Living

SOCRATES has been found guilty, and the penalty of death has been proposed. He has been asked to propose a counter-penalty. The wisdom, as well as the nobility and heroism, of his reply would have made him immortal if everything else he ever said had been lost. Even his accusers must have been forced to admit with Socrates that "the unexamined life is not worth living."

(From "The Apology")

SOCRATES   *And so he proposes death as the penalty. And what shall I propose on my part, O men of Athens? Clearly that which is my due. And what is my due? What return shall be made to the man who has never had the wit to be idle during his whole life; but has been careless of what the many care for—wealth, and family interests, and military offices, and speaking in the assembly, and magistracies, and plots, and parties. Reflecting that I was really too honest a man to be a politician and live, I did not go where I could do no good to you or to myself; but where I could do the greatest good privately to every one of you, thither I went, and sought to persuade every man among you that he must look to himself, and seek virtue and wisdom before he looks to his private interests, and look to the state before he looks to the interests of the state; and that this should be the order which he observes in all his actions. What shall be done to such an one? Doubtless some good thing, O men of Athens, if he has his reward; and the good should be of a kind suitable to him. What would be a reward suitable to a poor man who is your benefactor, and who desires leisure that he may instruct you? There can be no reward so fitting as maintenance in the Prytaneum, O men of Athens, a reward which he deserves far more than the*

24

citizen who has won the prize at Olympia in the horse or chariot race, whether the chariots were drawn by two horses or by many. For I am in want, and he has enough; and he only gives you the appearance of happiness, and I give you the reality. And if I am to estimate the penalty fairly, I should say that maintenance in the Prytaneum is the just return.

Perhaps you think that I am braving you in what I am saying now, as in what I said before about the tears and prayers. But this is not so. I speak rather because I am convinced that I never intentionally wronged any one, although I cannot convince you—the time has been too short; if there were a law at Athens, as there is in other cities, that a capital cause should not be decided in one day, then I believe that I should have convinced you. But I cannot in a moment refute great slanders; and, as I am convinced that I never wronged another, I will assuredly not wrong myself. I will not say of myself that I deserve any evil, or propose any penalty. Why should I? Because I am afraid of the penalty of death which Meletus proposes? When I do not know whether death is a good or an evil, why should I propose a penalty which would certainly be an evil? Shall I say imprisonment? And why should I live in prison, and be the slave of the magistrates of the year—of the Eleven? Or shall the penalty be a fine, and imprisonment until the fine is paid? There is the same objection. I should have to lie in prison, for money I have none, and cannot pay. And if I say exile (and this may possibly be the penalty which you will affix), I must indeed be blinded by the love of life, if I am so irrational as to expect that when you, who are my own citizens, cannot endure my discourses and words, and have found them so grievous and odious that you will have no more of them, others are likely to endure me. No indeed, men of Athens, that is not very likely. And what a life should I lead, at my age, wandering from city to city, ever changing my place of exile, and always being driven out!

Some one will say: Yes, Socrates, but cannot you hold your tongue, and then you may go into a foreign city,

*and no one will interfere with you? Now I have great
difficulty in making you understand my answer to this.
For if I tell you that to do as you say would be a dis-
obedience to the God, and therefore that I cannot hold
my tongue, you will not believe that I am serious; and
if I say again that daily to discourse about virtue, and
of those other things about which you hear me examining
myself and others, is the greatest good of man, and
that the unexamined life is not worth living, you are
still less likely to believe me.*

Socrates is asked to propose a counter-penalty to the
death sentence which has been demanded by his accusers. Had he been willing to cringe before his accusers, and thus, in effect, repudiate his life's work, they
would have been happy to agree to a lesser punishment.

Socrates was well aware that his friends were prepared to pay any sum of money which he might have
proposed as an alternative fine. It was not because he
wanted to spare his friends a loss of money, which he
knew they could easily afford, that he refused this way
of escape. He could not propose a fine or any other
penalty, without thereby pleading guilty; and this he
could not do without repudiating and betraying the
principles to which his life had been dedicated.

And as for either holding his tongue, or going into
exile, both were equally unthinkable.

For Socrates to agree to "cease and desist" would
have been equivalent to his acknowledging that his life
had been spent in a mission which was inimical to the
state and had accomplished nothing but harm.

Socrates, however, was convinced that his ideas were
not only worth living for, but worth dying for as well.
And even the divine voice within him, which had never
failed to correct him when he was wrong, assented now
by remaining silent.

Nor would exile have been preferable to death. It is
true that for an old man, a life of exile would hardly be
pleasant, but an ordinary man would hardly be expected
to choose death rather than exile, as Socrates did.

The real issue was not so much the fate of Socrates, but the fate of the freedom of ideas. Instead of pleading for his own life, Socrates presented the case for freedom, and documented his argument with his own life. What man could do more?

Not Even God Can Alter The Good

EUTHYPHRO, a young religious fanatic, is demonstrating to Athens and the world the superiority of his knowledge of the laws of man and God. On the strength of a far-fetched technicality, he is prosecuting his father for murder. His insufferable conceit and smugness, and his imperviousness to the ironic barbs of Socrates, are in dramatic contrast to the high-mindedness of Socrates and the sublimity of the great idea which is suggested in the overtones and implications of the dialogue.

(From the "Euthyphro")

SOCRATES *And what is your suit,* EUTHYPHRO? *Are you the pursuer or the defendant?*

EUTHYPHRO *I am the pursuer.*

SOC. *Of whom?*

EUTH. *You will think me mad when I tell you.*

SOC. *Why, has the fugitive wings?*

EUTH. *Nay, he is not very volatile at his time of life.*

SOC. *Who is he?*

EUTH. *My father.*

SOC. *Your father! my good man?*

EUTH. *Yes.*

SOC. *And of what is he accused?*

EUTH. *Of murder,* SOCRATES.

SOC. *By the powers,* EUTHYPHRO! *how little does the common herd know of the nature of right and truth. A man must be an extraordinary man, and must have made great strides in wisdom, before he could have seen his way to bring such an action.*

EUTH. *Indeed,* SOCRATES, *he must.*

SOC. *I suppose that the man whom your father murdered was one of your relatives—clearly he was; for if he had been a stranger you would never have thought of prosecuting him.*

28

EUTH. *I am amused,* SOCRATES, *at your making a distinction between one who is a relation and one who is not a relation; for surely the pollution is the same in either case, if you knowingly associate with the murderer when you ought to clear yourself and him by proceeding against him. The real question is whether the murdered man has been justly slain. If justly, then your duty is to let the matter alone; but, if unjustly then even if the murderer lives under the same roof with you and eats at the same table, proceed against him. Now the man who is dead was a poor dependent of mine who worked for us as a field laborer on our farm in Naxos, and one day in a fit of drunken passion he got into a quarrel with one of our domestic servants and slew him. My father bound him hand and foot and threw him into a ditch, and then sent to Athens to ask of a diviner what he should do with him. Meanwhile he never attended to him and took no care about him, for he regarded him as a murderer; and thought that no great harm would be done even if he did die. Now this was just what happened. For such was the effect of cold and hunger and chains upon him, that before the messenger returned from the diviner, he was dead. And my father and family are angry with me for taking the part of the murderer and prosecuting my father. They say that he did not kill him, and that if he did, the dead man was but a murderer, and I ought not to take any notice, for that a son is impious who prosecutes a father. Which shows,* SOCRATES, *how little they know what the gods think about piety and impiety.*

SOC. *Good heavens,* EUTHYPHRO! *and is your knowledge of religion and of things pious and impious so very exact, that, supposing the circumstances to be as you state them, you are not afraid lest you too may be doing an impious thing in bringing an action against your father?*

EUTH. *The best of* EUTHYPHRO, *and that which distinguishes him,* SOCRATES, *from other men, is his exact knowledge of all such matters. What should I be good for without it?*

SOC. *Rare friend! I think that I cannot do better than be your disciple.*

SOC. *Well, then, my dear friend* EUTHYPHRO, *do tell me, for my better instruction and information, what proof have you that in the opinion of all the gods a servant who is guilty of murder, and is put in chains by the master of the dead man, and dies because he is put in chains before he who bound him can learn from the interpreters of the gods what he ought to do with him, dies unjustly; and that on behalf of such an one a son ought to proceed against his father and accuse him of murder. How would you show that all the Gods absolutely agree in approving his act? Prove to me that they do, and I will applaud your wisdom as long as I live.*

EUTH. *It will be a difficult task; but I could make the matter very clear indeed to you.*

SOC. *I understand; you mean to say that I am not so quick of apprehension as the judges: for to them you will be sure to prove that the act is unjust, and hateful to the gods.*

EUTH. *Yes indeed,* SOCRATES; *at least if they will listen to me.*

SOC. *But they will be sure to listen if they find that you are a good speaker. There was a notion that came into my mind while you were speaking; I said to myself: 'Well, and what if* EUTHYPHRO *does prove to me that all the gods regarded the death of the serf as unjust, how do I know anything more of the nature of piety and impiety? for granting that this action may be hateful to the gods, still piety and impiety are not adequately defined by these distinctions, for that which is hateful to the gods has been shown to be also pleasing and dear to them.' And therefore,* EUTHYPHRO, *I do not ask you to prove this; I will suppose, if you like, that all the gods condemn and abominate such an action. But I will amend the definition so far as to say that what all the gods hate is impious, and what they love pious or holy; and what some of them love and others hate is both or neither. Shall this be our definition of piety and impiety?*

EUTH. *Why not,* SOCRATES?

SOC. *Why not! Certainly, as far as I am concerned,* EUTHY-PHRO, *there is no reason why not. But whether this admis-*

*sion will greatly assist you in the task of instructing me
as you promised, is a matter for you to consider.*

EUTH. *Yes, I should say that what all the gods love is
pious and holy, and the opposite which they all hate,
impious.*

SOC. *Ought we to inquire into the truth of this,* EUTHY-
PHRO, *or simply to accept the mere statement on our own
authority and that of others? What do you say?*

EUTH. *We should inquire; and I believe that the statement
will stand the test of inquiry.*

SOC. *We shall know better, my good friend, in a little
while. The point which I should first wish to understand
is whether the pious or holy is beloved by the gods because it is holy, or holy because it is beloved of the gods.*

EUTH. *I do not understand your meaning,* SOCRATES.

Euthyphro is the eternal blue-nose, the kind of person
whose fanaticism blinds him to every consideration of
common sense, and to the values of everyday living.

The mark of the confirmed fanatic is the overwhelming
conceit of his omniscience, his ability to know instantly
what is right and what is wrong.

Only a man who thinks that he knows all there is to
know about morals and religion could proceed with
such unbounded confidence in the rightness of his actions
as Euthyphro does.

When, with his characteristic needling irony, Socrates suggests that since Euthyphro knows so much about
the matters they are discussing, Socrates could do no
better than to become his disciple, Euthyphro, completely
oblivious to the irony, agrees.

For Socrates, the eternal verities, or, in the phrase
of Whitehead, "enduring objects," are the moral virtues:
goodness, piety, and holiness, which are also truth and
beauty.

These are beyond the reach of the gods themselves.

The question that Euthyphro did not understand goes
to the very foundations of the idealism of Socrates and
Plato. The good is not made good because the gods
love it, the gods love it because it is good in itself.

The same is true of the true, and the beautiful, and the holy. They are immutable, and eternal, and the gods themselves cannot change them.

The issue whether goods are intrinsic, or whether they are divine commandments, has been disputed to the present day. Some critics have felt that the basic teaching of the dialogue is contained in a remark not quoted above, that religion should rather be thought of as the cooperation of man with God towards some noble result. When a human action is performed, which is right, then no god could have done better; nor, on the other hand, is a wrong action excusable even if a god performs it.

Religion, like philosophy, is a rational and reasonable way of life; and the only commandments a true god can make are those which are intrinsically right.

The "Euthyphro," like the typical Socratic dialogue, ends without reaching a positive conclusion. Its value rests in its provocative character, that is, in the manner in which it spurs and prods the intellect.

The true, the good, and the beautiful are higher in authority than the divinity of the gods. Actions are right or wrong, regardless of whether they are performed by men or gods. If a god chooses to do evil, his action is no more excusable or right than if he were a man. The gods are not beyond good and evil; a true god will choose the good, while a god who chooses evil is an evil god and his action is evil.

These are some of the conclusions and implications which can be suggested to the reader's mind by the provocative experience of reading the "Euthyphro," even though the dialogue ends without reaching a positive conclusion, in the fashion of the typical Socratic dialogue, whose value is found in its suggestiveness rather than in a dogmatic preachment.

Can Virtue Be Taught?

MENO, a young Thessalian, questions Socrates on whether virtue can be taught, or whether it is acquired by practice. The question, however, cannot be answered before we know what virtue itself is.

(From the "Meno")

MENO *Can you tell me,* SOCRATES, *whether virtue is acquired by teaching or by practice; or if neither by teaching nor by practice, then whether it comes to a man by nature, or in what other way?*

SOCRATES MENO, *there was a time when the Thessalians were famous among the other Hellenes only for their riches and their riding; but now, if I am not mistaken, they are equally famous for their wisdom, especially at Larisa, which is the native city of your friend Aristippus.*

How different is our lot, my dear MENO! *Here at Athens there is a dearth of the commodity, and all wisdom seems to have emigrated from us to you. For literally I do not know what virtue is, and much less whether it is acquired by teaching or not.*

MENO *But are you in earnest,* SOCRATES, *in saying that you do not know what virtue is? And am I to carry back this report of you to Thessaly?*

SOC. *Not only that, my dear boy, but you may say further that I have never known of any one else who did, in my judgment.*

MENO *Then you have never met Georgias when he was at Athens.*

SOC. *By the Gods,* MENO, *be generous, and tell me what you say that virtue is; for I shall be truly delighted to find that I have been mistaken, and that you and Georgias do really have this knowledge; although I have been*

33

just saying that I have never found anybody who had.

MENO *There will be no difficulty, SOCRATES, in answering your question. Let us take first the virtue of a man—he should know how to administer the state, and in the administration of it to benefit his friends and to harm his enemies; and he must also be careful not to suffer harm himself. A woman's virtue, if you wish to know about that, may also be easily described: her duty is to order her house, and keep what is indoors, and obey her husband. Every age, every condition of life, young or old, male or female, bond or free, has a different virtue; there are virtues numberless, and no lack of definitions of them; for virtue is relative to the actions and ages of each of us in all that we do. And the same may be said of vice, SOCRATES.*

SOC. *How fortunate I am, MENO! When I ask you for one virtue you present me with a swarm of them, which are in your keeping. Suppose that I carry on the figure of the swarm, and ask of you, What is the nature of the bee? and you answer that there are many different kinds of bees, and I reply: But do bees differ as bees, because there are many and different kinds of them; or are they not rather to be distinguished by some other quality, as for example beauty, size or shape? How would you answer me?*

MENO *I should answer that bees do not differ from one another, as bees.*

SOC. *And if I went on to say: That is what I desire to know, MENO; tell me what is the quality in which they do not differ, but are all alike;—would you be able to answer?*

MENO *I should.*

SOC. *And so of the virtues, however many and different they may be, they have all a common nature which makes them virtues; and on this he who would answer the question, 'What is virtue?' would do well to have his eye fixed: Do you understand?*

MENO *I am beginning to understand; but I do not as yet take hold of the question as I could wish.*

Once again we see Socrates in his role of ironic modesty and profound ignorance. The dialogue begins with the question of whether virtue is acquired by teaching or by practice. But this question cannot be answered without first knowing what virtue is.

Noteworthy in this citation is Socrates' insistence upon the necessity of stating the common essence of a term which is to be defined. A swarm of examples will not do, as Socrates points out to Meno in a lesson in elementary logic for which the dialogue is famous. It is not enough to offer examples of the term being defined. The common essence which unites the examples must be understood and specifically stated.

Aristotle, who was himself a pupil of Plato, later formalized the distinction made by Socrates by distinguishing between a definition which merely listed examples and one which stated the common essence which the examples shared. He named the former a statement of the *extension* of the term, and the latter a statement of the *intension* of the term.

The dialogue reaffirms the firm conviction of Socrates that the virtues are one.

Plato does not hesitate to introduce his own ideas through the device of having Socrates speak them, and as the dialogue proceeds, Plato introduces his own characteristic theory of education—the doctrine of reminiscence—that education consists of drawing out from a pupil that which he already knows, thus, that education is recollection.

Education Is Recollection

THE INCOMPARABLE SKILL of Socrates as a teacher is demonstrated by the vivid example of his art which Plato has recreated for us in the "Meno."

The method of teaching which Socrates uses here has served as the model and inspiration for the best teachers of every generation from ancient times to this very day. In his honor it is still known as the Socratic method.

Socrates believed that learning was a creative process, in which a teacher served as midwife at the birth of his pupil's ideas, rather than as a nurse feeding an infant with a spoon.

(From the "Meno")

MENO *Yes,* SOCRATES; *but what do you mean by saying that we do not learn, and that what we call learning is only a process of recollection? Can you teach me how this is?*

SOCRATES *I told you,* MENO, *just now that you were a rogue, and now you ask whether I can teach you, when I am saying that there is no teaching, but only recollection; and thus you imagine that you will involve me in a contradiction.*

MENO *Indeed,* SOCRATES, *I protest that I had no such intention. I only asked the question from habit; but if you can prove to me that what you say is true, I wish that you would.*

SOC. *It will be no easy matter, but I will try to please you to the utmost of my power. Suppose that you call one of your numerous attendants, that I may demonstrate on him.*

MENO *Certainly. Come hither, boy.*

SOC. *He is Greek, and speaks Greek, does he not?*

MENO *Yes, indeed; he was born in the house.*

36

soc. *Attend now to the questions which I ask him, and observe whether he learns of me or only remembers.*

meno *I will.*

soc. *Tell me, boy, do you know that a figure like this is a square?*

boy *I do.*

soc. *And you know that a square figure has these four lines equal?*

boy *Certainly.*

soc. *And these lines which I have drawn through the middle of the square are also equal?*

boy *Yes.*

soc. *A square may be of any size?*

boy *Certainly.*

soc. *And if one side of the figure be of two feet, and the other side be of two feet, how much will the whole be? Let me explain: if in one direction the space was of two feet, and in the other direction of one foot, the whole would be of two feet taken once?*

boy *Yes.*

soc. *But since this side is also of two feet, there are twice two feet?*

boy *There are.*

soc. *Then the square is of twice two feet?*

boy *Yes.*

soc. *And how many are twice two feet? count and tell me.*

boy *Four,* socrates.

soc. *And might there not be another square twice as large as this, and having like this the lines equal?*

boy *Yes.*

soc. *And of how many feet will that be?*

boy *Of eight feet.*

soc. *And now try and tell me the length of the line which forms the side of that double square: this is two feet—what will that be?*

boy *Clearly,* socrates, *it will be double.*

soc. *Do you observe,* meno, *that I am not teaching the boy anything, but only asking him questions; and now he fancies that he knows how long a line is necessary in order to produce a figure of eight square feet; does he not?*

MENO *Yes.*

SOC. *And does he really know?*

MENO *Certainly not.*

SOC. *He only guesses that because the square is double, the line is double.*

MENO *True.*

SOC. *Observe him while he recalls the steps in regular order. (To the Boy.) Tell me, boy, do you assert that a double space comes from a double line? Remember that I am not speaking of an oblong, but of a figure equal every way, and twice the size of this—that is to say of eight feet; and I want to know whether you still say that a double square comes from a double line?*

BOY *Yes.*

SOC. *But does not this line become doubled if we add another such line here?*

BOY *Certainly.*

SOC. *And four such lines will make a space containing eight feet?*

BOY *Yes.*

SOC. *Let us describe such a figure: Would you not say that this is the figure of eight feet?*

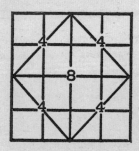

BOY *Yes.*

SOC. *And are there not these four divisions in the figure, each of which is equal to the figure of four feet?*

BOY *True.*

SOC. *And is not that four times four?*

BOY *Certainly.*

SOC. *And four times is not double?*

BOY *No, indeed.*

SOC. *But how much?*

BOY *Four times as much.*

SOC. *Therefore the double line, boy, has given a space, not twice, but four times as much.*

BOY *True.*

SOC. *Four times four are sixteen—are they not?*

BOY *Yes.*

SOC. *What line would give you a space of eight feet, as this gives one of sixteen feet—do you see?*

BOY *Yes.*

SOC. *And the space of four feet is made from this half line?*

BOY *Yes.*

SOC. *Good; and is not a space of eight feet twice the size of this, and half the size of the other?*

BOY *Certainly.*

SOC. *Such a space, then, will be made out of a line greater than this one, and less than that one?*

BOY *Yes; I think so.*

SOC. *Very good; I like to hear you say what you think. And now tell me, is not this a line of two feet and that of four?*

BOY *Yes.*

SOC. *Then the line which forms the side of eight feet ought to be more than this line of two feet, and less than the other of four feet?*

BOY *It ought.*

SOC. *Try and see if you can tell me how much it will be.*

BOY *Three feet.*

SOC. *Then if we add a half to this line of two, that will be the line of three. Here are two and there is one; and on the other side, here are two also and there is one: and that makes the figure of which you speak?*

BOY *Yes.*

soc. *But if there are three feet this way and three feet that way, the whole space will be three times three feet?*

boy *That is evident.*

soc. *And how much are three times three feet?*

boy *Nine.*

soc. *And how much is the double of four?*

boy *Eight.*

soc. *Then the figure of eight is not made out of a line of three?*

boy *No.*

soc. *But from what line?—tell me exactly; and if you would rather not reckon, try and show me the line.*

boy *Indeed,* socrates, *I do not know.*

soc. *Do you see,* meno, *what advances he has made in his power of recollection? He did not know at first, and he does not know now, what is the side of a figure of eight feet: but then he thought that he knew, and answered confidently as if he knew, and had no difficulty; now he has a difficulty, and neither knows nor fancies that he knows.*

meno *True.*

soc. *Is he not better off in knowing his ignorance?*

meno *I think that he is.*

soc. *If we have made him doubt, and given him the 'torpedo's shock,' have we done him any harm?*

meno *I think not.*

soc. *We have certainly, as would seem, assisted him in some degree to the discovery of the truth; and now he will wish to remedy his ignorance, but then he would have been ready to tell all the world again and again that the double space should have a double side.*

meno *True.*

soc. *But do you suppose that he would ever have enquired into or learned what he fancied that he knew, though he was really ignorant of it, until he had fallen into perplexity under the idea that he did not know, and had desired to know?*

meno *I think not,* socrates.

soc. *Then he was the better for the torpedo's touch?*

MENO *I think so.*

SOC. *Mark now the farther development. I shall only ask him, and not teach him, and he shall share the inquiry with me: and do you watch and see if you find me telling or explaining anything to him, instead of eliciting his opinion. Tell me, boy, is not this a square of four feet which I have drawn?*

BOY *Yes.*

SOC. *And now I add another square equal to the former one?*

BOY *Yes.*

SOC. *And a third, which is equal to either of them?*

BOY *Yes.*

SOC. *Suppose that we fill up the vacant corner?*

BOY *Very good.*

SOC. *Here, then, there are four equal spaces?*

BOY *Yes.*

SOC. *And how many times larger is this space than this other?*

BOY *Four times.*

SOC. *But it ought to have been twice only, as you will remember.*

BOY *True.*

SOC. *And does not this line, reaching from corner to corner, bisect each of these spaces?*

BOY *Yes.*

SOC. *And are there not here four equal lines which contain this space?*

BOY *There are.*

SOC. *Look and see how much this space is.*

BOY *I do not understand.*

SOC. *Has not each interior line cut off half of the four spaces?*

BOY *Yes.*

SOC. *And how many spaces are there in this section?*

BOY *Four.*

SOC. *And how many in this?*

BOY *Two.*

SOC. *And four is how many times two?*

BOY *Twice.*

SOC. *And this space is of how many feet?*

BOY *Of eight feet.*

SOC. *And from what line do you get this figure?*

BOY *From this.*

SOC. *That is, from the line which extends from corner to corner of the figure of four feet?*

BOY *Yes.*

SOC. *And that is the line which the learned call the diagonal. And if this is the proper name, then you, Meno's slave, are prepared to affirm that the double space is the square of the diagonal?*

BOY *Certainly,* SOCRATES.

SOC. *What do you say of him,* MENO? *Were not all these answers given out of his own head?*

MENO *Yes, they were all his own.*

SOC. *And yet, as we were just now saying, he did not know?*

MENO *True.*

SOC. *But still he had in him those notions of his—had he not?*

MENO *Yes.*

SOC. *Then he who does not know may still have true notions of that which he does not know?*

MENO *He has.*

SOC. *And at present these notions have just been stirred up in him, as in a dream; but if he were frequently asked the same questions, in different forms, he would know as well as any one at last?*

MENO *I dare say.*

SOC. *Without any one teaching him he will recover his knowledge for himself, if he is only asked questions?*

MENO *Yes.*

SOC. *And this spontaneous recovery of knowledge in him is recollection?*

MENO *True.*

SOC. *And this knowledge which he now has must he not either have acquired or always possessed?*

MENO *Yes.*

SOC. *But if he always possessed this knowledge he would always have known; or if he has acquired the knowl-*

edge he could not have acquired it in this life, unless he has been taught geometry; for he may be made to do the same with all geometry and every other branch of knowledge. Now, has any one ever taught him all this? You must know about him, if, as you say, he was born and bred in your house.

MENO *And I am certain that no one ever did teach him.*

SOC. *And yet he has the knowledge?*

MENO *The fact, SOCRATES, is undeniable.*

SOC. *But if he did not acquire the knowledge in this life, then he must have had and learned it at some other time?*

MENO *Clearly he must.*

SOC. *Which must have been the time when he was not a man?*

MENO *Yes.*

SOC. *And if there have been always true thoughts in him, both at the time when he was and was not a man, which only need to be awakened into knowledge by putting questions to him, his soul must have always possessed this knowledge, for he always either was or was not a man?*

MENO *Obviously.*

SOC. *And if the truth of all things always existed in the soul, then the soul is immortal. Wherefore be of good cheer, and try to recollect what you do not know, or rather what you do not remember.*

MENO *I feel, somehow, that I like what you are saying.*

SOC. *And I, MENO, like what I am saying. Some things I have said of which I am not altogether confident. But that we shall be better and braver and less helpless if we think that we ought to inquire, than we should have been if we indulged in the idle fancy that there was no knowing and no use in seeking to know what we do not know;—that is a theme upon which I am ready to fight, in word and deed, to the utmost of my power.*

In the "Meno," as in many of the dialogues, Plato intermingles his own teachings with those of Socrates as though the teachings of master and pupil were one.

The Plato scholars of the world still dispute over the fine points of separating the contributions of Socrates from those of Plato himself. They all agree, however, that the doctrine of "forms" or "ideas" (See Chapters 18,27,28,29) which is briefly introduced in the "Meno," is purely Platonic. This is conclusively demonstrated by those dialogues in which the personality of Socrates is omitted or subordinated and in which the doctrine of forms is made central. In the "Symposium," for example, Plato permits his own ideas to be identified as non-Socratic by attributing them to a fictitious wise woman Diotima (See Chapters 28 and 29).

The principal charm of the "Meno" for the beginner is found in the vividness of the portrayal of Socrates, the teacher, and in the significance of the lesson that it teaches about the nature and purpose of education.

The very words "education" and "instruction" testify to the fact that Socrates' theory of education has become woven into the fabric of our thought.

"Instruction" is derived from the Latin "instruere" which means "to build on."

"Education" is derived from the Latin "educare" which means "to lead forth."

Instruction then signifies the process whereby the instructor puts his own thoughts into the minds of his pupils by drill and rote methods.

Education on the contrary refers to the process whereby an educator "leads forth" from the mind of his pupil the thoughts that his own student has created by the activity of his own thinking. The educator then is the teacher who makes his own students think.

Pupils who have been trained by instructors rather than educators do not understand the creative powers of thought. They do not know what it means to make intelligent guesses. The only time they do guess is when they know they should not. This is when they are attempting to reproduce facts which they have forgotten.

A student who has been trained by an educator learns to make intelligent guesses—not about facts where guessing is stupid—but in evaluating the significance of facts.

Who Are Your Friends?

LYSIS, young and handsome scion of a noted Athenian family, is a young gentleman who can boast of many friends. For that reason Socrates urges him to clarify the real meaning of friendship. Lysis is clearly unequal to the task, and his friend, Menexenus, who is slightly older and whose mind is more subtle, does not fare much better. Socrates convincingly demonstrates that while they are all friends, none of them can express what friendship is.

(From the "Lysis")

SOCRATES *Very well, I said, I will; and do you, MENEXENUS, answer. But first I must tell you that I am one who from my childhood upward have set my heart upon a certain thing. All people have their fancies; some desire horses, and others dogs; and some are fond of gold, and others of honor. Now, I have no violent desire of any of these things; but I have a passion for friends; and I would rather have a good friend than the best cock or quail in the world: I would even go further, and say the best horse or dog. Yea, by the dog of Egypt, I should greatly prefer a real friend to all the gold of Darius, or even to Darius himself: I am such a lover of friends as that. And when I see you and Lysis, at your early age, so easily possessed of this treasure, and so soon, he of you, and you of him, I am amazed and delighted, seeing that I myself, although I am now advanced in years, am so far from having made a similar acquisition, that I do not even know in what way a friend is acquired. But I want to ask you a question about this, for you have experience: tell me then, when one loves another, is the lover or the beloved the friend; or may either be the friend?*

45

MENEXENUS *Either may, I should think, be the friend of either.*

soc. *Do you mean, I said, that if only one of them loves the other, they are mutual friends?*

MEN. *Yes, he said; that is my meaning.*

soc. *But what if the lover is not loved in return? which is a very possible case.*

MEN. *Yes.*

soc. *Or is, perhaps, even hated? which is a fancy which sometimes is entertained by lovers respecting their beloved. Nothing can exceed their love; and yet they imagine either that they are not loved in return, or that they are hated. Is not that true?*

MEN. *Yes, he said, quite true.*

soc. *In that case, the one loves, and the other is loved?*

MEN. *Yes.*

soc. *Then which is the friend of which? Is the lover the friend of the beloved, whether he be loved in return, or hated; or is the beloved the friend; or is there no friendship at all on either side, unless they both love one another?*

MEN. *There would seem to be none at all.*

soc. *Then this notion is not in accordance with our previous one. We were saying that both were friends, if one only loved; but now, unless they both love, neither is a friend.*

MEN. *That appears to be true.*

soc. *Then nothing which does not love in return is beloved by a lover?*

MEN. *I think not.*

soc. *Then they are not lovers of horses, whom the horses do not love in return; nor lovers of quails, nor of dogs, nor of wine, nor of gymnastic exercises, who have no return of love; no, nor of wisdom, unless wisdom loves them in return. Or shall we say that they do love them, although they are not beloved by them; and that the poet was wrong who sings—*

'Happy the man to whom his children are dear, and steeds having single hoofs, and dogs of chase, and the stranger of another land'?

MEN. *I do not think that he was wrong.*

SOC. *You think that he is right?*

MEN. *Yes.*

SOC. *Then,* MENEXENUS, *the conclusion is, that what is beloved, whether loving or hating, may be dear to the lover of it: for example, very young children, too young to love, or even hating their father or mother when they are punished by them, are never dearer to them than at the time when they are being hated by them.*

MEN. *I think that what you say is true.*

SOC. *And, if so, not the lover, but the beloved, is the friend or dear one?*

MEN. *Yes.*

SOC. *And the hated one, and not the hater, is the enemy?*

MEN. *Clearly.*

SOC. *Then many men are loved by their enemies, and hated by their friends, and are the friends of their enemies, and the enemies of their friends. Yet how absurd, my dear friend, or indeed impossible is this paradox of a man being an enemy to his friend or a friend to his enemy.*

The principal idea behind this selection is that friendship requires mutuality. One-sided friendships are really not friendships at all.

Socrates, in developing the argument, explores the possible relationships which are significant in accounting for a friendship. Here is a brief summary of the dialogue.

Menexenus begins the discussion of the meaning of friendship by suggesting that *friendship must involve a mutual relationship,* to which Socrates objects by pointing out that wine and wisdom cannot love back.

To this Menexenus replies: In that case, *it must be the beloved who is the friend;* which draws the objection from Socrates that when I punish a child because I love him and want to make him better, then according to Menexenus he is my friend because he is my beloved. But suppose he hates me because I am punishing him. Then my friend is the person who hates me, and I am also his enemy, because he hates me. This resolves into the absurdity that when a parent loves a child who hates the parent, then the parent is being hated by a friend, and the child is being loved by an enemy.

Menexenus then proposes the alternative that *it is the lover who is the friend.*

Socrates immediately points out that the previous paradox will hold, just as it did before, if the one whom the lover loves hates him in return.

To which Menexenus replies: *The like, or the similar, are friends.*

Socrates' objection to this view is that bad men cannot be friends, because the closer they get, the more hostile they are. Therefore only the good can be friends.

Furthermore, if good men are friends, they must be good in different ways, because like things cannot affect each other. For one thing to interest another, there must be enough difference to cause a reaction (e.g. water does not act on water).

Therefore if the good are friends, the reason for their friendship is their goodness, not their likeness.

But a friend can have no value for a good man, since in proportion as a man is good, he is self-sufficient.

Menexenus then suggests that *the unlike are friends.*

Socrates, objecting, replies: Then a man would love those who detest him, the temperate and the profligate would be friends, which is impossible.

Menexenus tries again: *The good and the neutral (neither good nor bad) are friends.*

Socrates objects, of course, and says: Anything which is not yet actually evil will strive for the good. The very presence of evil makes it desire the corresponding good. Thus the neutral is friendly to that which is good because it wants to escape from that which is bad, and is friendly for the sake of that which is good.

This implies that whatever is desired is desired for the sake of something else; but there must be something which is desired for its own sake.

However, if we care for good in order to escape from evil, then we would not care for the good if there were no evil. But this could not be because we would still care for food even if it were not harmful to the hungry, that is, for the pleasures of eating.

Menexenus makes one final attempt: *The friend is that which is desired when it is desired.*

Socrates disposes of Menexenus' last try by objecting that: A person desires that in which he is deficient, which he feels he needs in order to be fully himself. Real friends are parts of each other in soul, temper, or body, and they belong to each other. Therefore, friendship must be mutual and reciprocal.

But this was disproven in the first argument.

Thus the dialogue ends in a circle.

1. If what belongs to a man is also what is like a man, then the proof that the like cannot be friends is contradicted.

2. If what belongs to a man is different from the man, then since good things belong to each other on account of their goodness, bad on account of their badness, and neutral on account of their neutralness, this contradicts the conclusion that the bad cannot be friends.

3. Or if what belongs to a person is his good, then friends must be both good, which was disproven.

Throughout the dialogue the prevading theme which cuts through all the tricks of the dialectical contradictions is the insistence that the good is the basic tie between friends, and that which makes friendships possible.

The quality, or degree, of a friendship, is proportional to the quality or degree of good, which unites the friends. We are only too familiar with the person who is friendly only for ulterior reasons, who makes friends only for what his "friends" can do for him. The quality of his friendship is as meager as the advantages that he can wheedle from his "connections."

In a true friendship, there is mutual affection, and regard, and the friend is loved for his own sake, not for any external advantages which may accrue from the friendship. Friendship is a virtue, and the virtues are ultimately one, namely, the good; and the good is an end in itself, which is desired only for its own sake.

Temperance And Headaches

CHARMIDES, a young nobleman, and Plato's uncle, is
celebrated for his modesty and his temperance. He is
suffering from a headache, but before his body can be
properly treated Socrates must find out whether his soul
is in order, that is whether he possesses the virtue of temperance, and can explain what it means. Since Charmides
is himself a model of temperance, this should not be too
difficult. The reader is not surprised to discover that he
is no match for Socrates.

(From the "Charmides")

SOCRATES   *Hear, then, I said, my own dream; whether
coming through the horn or the ivory gate, I cannot tell.
The dream is this: Let us suppose that wisdom is such as
we are now defining, and that she has absolute sway over
us; then each action will be done according to the arts
or sciences, and no one professing to be a pilot when he
is not, or any physician or general, or any one else pre-
tending to know matters of which he is ignorant, will
deceive or elude us; our health will be improved; our
safety at sea, and also in battle, will be assured; our
coats and shoes, and all other instruments and implements will be skilfully made, because the workmen will
be good and true. Aye, and if you please, you may
suppose that prophecy, which is the knowledge of the
future, will be under the control of wisdom, and that
she will deter deceivers and set up the true prophets in
their place as the revealers of the future. Now I quite
agree that mankind, thus provided, would live and act
according to knowledge, for wisdom would watch and
prevent ignorance from intruding on us. But whether by
acting according to knowledge we shall act well and be*

50

happy, my dear CRITIAS,—*this is a point which we have not yet been able to determine.*

CRITIAS *Yes I think, he replied, that if you discard knowledge, you will hardly find the crown of happiness in anything else.*

SOC. *But of what is this knowledge? I said. Just answer me that small question. Do you mean a knowledge of shoemaking?*

CRIT. *God forbid.*

SOC. *Or of working in brass?*

CRIT. *Certainly not.*

SOC. *Or in wool, or wood, or anything of that sort?*

CRIT. *No, I do not.*

SOC. *Then, I said, we are giving up the doctrine that he who lives according to knowledge is happy, for these live according to knowledge, and yet they are not allowed by you to be happy; but I think that you mean to confine happiness to particular individuals who live according to knowledge, such for example as the prophet, who, as I was saying, knows the future. Is it of him you are speaking or of some one else?*

CRIT. *Yes, I mean him, but there are others as well.*

SOC. *Yes, I said, some one who knows the past and present as well as the future, and is ignorant of nothing. Let us suppose that there is such a person, and if there is, you will allow that he is the most knowing of all living men.*

CRIT. *Certainly he is.*

SOC. *Yet I should like to know one thing more: which of the different kinds of knowledge makes him happy? or do all equally make him happy?*

CRIT. *Not all equally, he replied.*

SOC. *But which most tends to make him happy? the knowledge of what past, present, or future thing? May I infer this to be the knowledge of the game of draughts?*

CRIT. *Nonsense about the game of draughts.*

SOC. *Or of computation?*

CRIT. *No.*

SOC. *Or of health?*

CRIT. *That is nearer the truth, he said.*

soc. *And that knowledge which is nearest of all, I said, is the knowledge of what?*

crit. *The knowledge with which he discerns good and evil.*

soc. *Monster! I said; you have been carrying me round in a circle, and all this time hiding from me the fact that the life according to knowledge is not that which makes men act rightly and be happy, not even if knowledge include all the sciences, but one science only, that of good and evil.*

The world has just begun to catch up to the problem posed by Plato in this selection from the "Charmides."

Let us suppose we have unlimited knowledge in all of the arts and sciences, except the science of good and evil. Would we, under those circumstances, act justly and be happy?

Are the arts and technology, no matter to what superlative degree they may be perfected, enough to insure right living and happiness?

"Impossible," says Plato.

We, who live in a world which is now beginning to make an inventory of the dangers, as well as the advantages, brought to us by technology, are forced to agree.

No longer do we feel entirely secure in a world run by engineers and politicians. We now know that we need social engineering and sound statesmanship as well.

That knowledge, without which all other knowledge for insuring happiness is inadequate, is the knowledge of good, the knowledge of right and wrong. This is, in effect, the science of relative values, in a scale leading to the final intrinsic good itself, the achievement of which is the only real happiness.

What good are all of the scientific advances of the past century, if we fail to work out, for ourselves, a way of life that will bring us the only valid fruits of all our knowledge.

The "Charmides" is concerned with the definition of one of the virtues, *sophrosyne*, which is translated approximately as temperance.

Charmides himself is a beautiful youth, who is noted for his equally beautiful character. Since in the actual conduct of his own life, he has proven himself to be the very model of temperance, he makes an appropriate respondent for Socrates in the quest for an understanding of the meaning of the word "temperance."

Who Is A Brave Man?

LACHES AND NICIAS are two famous generals who are being consulted by the sons of two Athenians, Aristides, the just, and Thucydides, the general-historian, for advice on the sort of education their own sons would require to become as distinguished as their grandfathers. The military experts find themselves at variance on the question, and Laches consults Socrates in order to obtain a decisive opinion. Socrates must first learn what is meant by courage.

(From the "Laches")

SOCRATES   *And I suppose I were to be asked by some one: What is that common quality, SOCRATES, which, in all these uses of the word, you call quickness? I should say the quality which accomplishes much in a little time —whether in running, speaking, or in any other sort of action.*

LACHES   *You would be quite correct.*

SOC.   *And now, LACHES, do you try and tell me in like manner, What is that common quality which is called courage, and which includes all the various uses of the term when applied both to pleasure and pain, and in all the cases to which I was just now referring?*

LA.   *I should say that courage is a sort of endurance of the soul, if I am to speak of the universal nature which pervades them all.*

SOC.   *But that is what we must do if we are to answer the question. And yet I cannot say that every kind of endurance is, in my opinion, to be deemed courage. Hear my reason: I am sure, LACHES, that you would consider courage to be a very noble quality.*

LA.   *Most noble, certainly.*

SOC.   *And you would say that a wise endurance is also good and noble?*

LA. *Very noble.*

SOC. *But what would you say of a foolish endurance? Is not that, on the other hand, to be regarded as evil and hurtful?*

LA. *True.*

SOC. *And is anything noble which is evil and hurtful?*

LA. *I ought not to say that,* SOCRATES.

SOC. *Then you would not admit that sort of endurance to be courage—for it is not noble, but courage is noble?*

LA. *You are right.*

SOC. *Then, according to you, only the wise endurance is courage?*

LA. *True.*

SOC. *But as to the epithet 'wise'—wise in what? In all things small as well as great? For example, if a man shows the quality of endurance in spending his money wisely, knowing that by spending he will acquire more in the end, do you call him courageous?*

LA. *Assuredly not.*

SOC. *Or, for example, if a man is a physician, and his son, or some patient of his, has inflammation of the lungs, and begs that he may be allowed to eat or drink something, and the other is firm and refuses; is that courage?*

LA. *No; that is not courage at all, any more than the last.*

SOC. *Again, take the case of one who endures in war, and is willing to fight, and wisely calculates and knows that others will help him, and that there will be fewer and inferior men against him than there are with him; and suppose that he has also advantages of position—would you say of such a one who endures with all this wisdom and preparation, that he, or some man in the opposing army who is in the opposite circumstances to these and yet endures and remains at his post, is the braver?*

LA. *I should say that the latter,* SOCRATES, *was the braver.*

SOC. *But, surely, this is a foolish endurance in comparison with the other?*

LA. *That is true.*

SOC. *Then you would say that he who in an engagement of cavalry endures, having the knowledge of horseman-*

*ship, is not so courageous as he who endures, having no
such knowledge?*

LA. So I should say.

SOC. *And he who endures, having a knowledge of the use
of the sling, or the bow, or of any other art, is not so
courageous as he who endures, not having such a knowledge?*

LA. *True.*

SOC. *And he who descends into a well, and dives, and
holds out in this or any similar action, having no knowledge of diving, or the like, is, as you would say, more
courageous than those who have this knowledge?*

LA. *Why, SOCRATES, what else can a man say?*

SOC. *Nothing, if that be what he thinks.*

LA. *But that is what I do think.*

SOC. *And yet men who thus run risks and endure are foolish, LACHES, in comparison of those who do the same
things, having the skill to do them.*

LA. *That is true.*

SOC. *But foolish boldness and endurance appeared before
to be base and hurtful to us.*

LA. *Quite true.*

SOC. *Whereas courage was acknowledged to be a noble
quality.*

LA. *True.*

SOC. *And now on the contrary we are saying that the
foolish endurance, which was before held in dishonor, is
courage.*

LA. *Very true.*

SOC. *And are we right in saying so?*

LA. *Indeed, SOCRATES, I am sure that we are not right.*

NICIAS   *Why, LACHES, I do not call animals or any other
things which have no fear of dangers, because they are
ignorant of them, courageous, but only fearless and
senseless. Do you imagine that I should call little children courageous, which fear no dangers because they
know none? There is a difference, to my way of thinking,
between fearlessness and courage. I am of opinion that
thoughtful courage is a quality possessed by very few,*

but that rashness and boldness, and fearlessness, which has no forethought, are very common qualities possessed by many men, many women, many children, many animals. And you, and men in general, call by the term 'courageous' actions which I call rash;—my courageous actions are wise actions.

Laches and Nicias were professional soldiers, and appropriately enough, since they were exemplars of the virtue of bravery, Socrates turns to them for enlightenment concerning the nature and meaning of bravery.

As in the preceding selections from the "Charmides" and "Lysis," Socrates skillfully involves his respondents in one contradiction after another as he spins his dialectic web around them. And the dialogue leads to no positive conclusion.

Courage turns out in the end to be the knowledge of both good and evil, and this includes all of the virtues. Thus, as in the "Charmides" and the "Lysis," Socrates skillfully presses home his point that the virtues are really one, the good.

Much of what is said about courage in the dialogue has lost the paradoxical flavor that it had when Socrates first made his investigations.

No longer are we surprised to discover that a man who is afraid, is braver than a man who is not afraid. The absence of fear is not courage in the literal sense, nor is courage the same as ignorance.

The man who knows and fears the consequences, and yet carries on either in, or beyond, the necessities of his duty, is obviously much braver than the man who is not afraid because he does not know the danger. Courage involves not only resoluteness of spirit, but the degree of courage is proportional to the relative degree of the risk involved which, in turn, depends upon two opposed factors:

(a) The less skill and training a person has, the greater the risk for him, and the greater the courage in meeting that risk. Here the greater the risk, the greater the courage.

(b)   The firmer a person's resolution to be brave, the less the risk that he will fail by going into a panic. Here the less risk, the greater the courage.

The brave man knows the danger. He knows his skill or lack of skill. He knows what is good and what is right. He is not afraid of the danger, but only of being afraid.

What Is The Source of Evil?

HIPPIAS is a well-known sophist of Elis, one of the itinerant teachers of ancient Greece. The sophists, in contrast to Socrates, were always professional teachers, and were typically conceited and dogmatic self-styled experts on any topic, no matter how little they might actually know about it. Socrates introduces the central paradox that a man who misses the mark on purpose is better than the man who misses it through lack of skill. He indirectly reaffirms his conviction that all wrong-doing is the result of ignorance.

(From the "Hippias Minor")

SOCRATES *Now,* HIPPIAS, *I think that I understand your meaning; when you say that Odysseus is wily, you clearly mean that he is false?*

HIPPIAS *Exactly so,* SOCRATES; *it is the character of Odysseus as he is represented by Homer in many passages both of the Iliad and Odyssey.*

SOC. *And Homer must be presumed to have meant that the true man is not the same as the false?*

HIP. *Of course,* SOCRATES.

SOC. *And is that your own opinion,* HIPPIAS?

HIP. *Certainly; how can I have any other?*

SOC. *Well, then, as there is no possibility of asking Homer what he meant in these verses of his, let us leave him; but as you show a willingness to take up his cause, and your opinion agrees with what you declare to be his, will you answer on behalf of yourself and him?*

HIP. *I will; ask shortly anything which you like.*

SOC. *Do you say that the false, like the sick, have no power to do things, or that they have the power to do things?*

HIP. *I should say that they have power to do many things, and in particular to deceive mankind.*

SOC. *Then, according to you, they are both powerful and wily, are they not?*

HIP. *Yes.*

SOC. *And are they wily, and do they deceive by reason of their simplicity and folly, or by reason of their cunning and a certain sort of prudence?*

HIP. *By reason of their cunning and prudence, most certainly.*

SOC. *Then they are prudent, I suppose?*

HIP. *So they are—very.*

SOC. *And if they are prudent, do they know or do they not know what they do?*

HIP. *Of course, they know very well; and that is why they do mischief to others.*

SOC. *And having this knowledge, are they ignorant, or are they wise?*

HIP. *Wise, certainly; at least, in so far as they can deceive.*

SOC. *Stop, and let us recall to mind what you are saying; are you not saying that the false are powerful and prudent and knowing and wise in those things about which they are false?*

HIP. *To be sure.*

SOC. *And the true differ from the false—the true and the false are the very opposite of each other?*

HIP. *That is my view.*

SOC. *Then, according to your view, it would seem that the false are to be ranked in the class of the powerful and wise?*

HIP. *Assuredly.*

SOC. *And when you say that the false are powerful and wise in so far as they are false, do you mean that they have or have not the power of uttering their falsehoods if they like?*

HIP. *I mean to say that they have the power.*

SOC. *In a word, then, the false are they who are wise and have the power to speak falsely?*

HIP. *Yes.*

SOC. *And tell me, HIPPIAS, are you not a skilful calculator and arithmetician?*

HIP. *Yes,* SOCRATES, *assuredly I am.*

SOC. *And if some one were to ask you what is the sum of 3 multiplied by 700 you would tell him the true answer in a moment, if you pleased?*

HIP. *Certainly I should.*

SOC. *Is not that because you are the wisest and ablest of men in these matters?*

HIP. *Yes.*

SOC. *And being as you are the wisest and ablest of men in these matters of calculation, are you not also the best?*

HIP. *To be sure,* SOCRATES, *I am the best.*

SOC. *And therefore you would be the most able to tell the truth about these matters, would you not?*

HIP. *Yes, I should.*

SOC. *And could you speak falsehoods about them equally well?*

SOC. *Then the good and wise geometer has this double power in the highest degree; and if there be a man who is false about diagrams the good man will be he, for he is able to be false; whereas the bad is unable, and for this reason is not false, as has been admitted.*

The principal paradox which Socrates defends in this dialogue is that the man who misses the mark on purpose is better, i.e., more skillful, than the man who misses the mark involuntarily. The man who knows the most about his own subject is the one can best mislead you about it. For example, he is a better mathematician than the one who might give false answers without knowing that they are false.

The real lesson in the dialogue is found, however, not in this paradox, the value of which lies in its affording Plato with an artistic, dramatic device of presenting his point indirectly and subtly, but with the electrifying effect typical of the Socratic dialectic.

Socrates is willing to grant the thesis of the paradox, but only for the sake of argument.

When Socrates agrees at the end of the citation that: "and if there be a man who is false about diagrams, the good man will be he," he is not asserting that there is such a man, rather he is warning us that he does not think there *could* be such a man.

If a man could do wrong on purpose, he would have to be a good man, because a bad man does not have the skill to do wrong on purpose, and only the good man has the skill.

It would be unthinkable, however, for the good man ever to have the wish to do wrong on purpose. And as for the bad man, not even he could ever do anything wrong except by mistake.

One of the greatest of the ideas taught by Socrates, and immortalized by Plato, is this very idea that no one can ever do anything wrong on purpose, that evil-doing is ignorance, and the man who knows can never do wrong.

No matter how depraved a person be, he chooses that action which he thinks is good for himself, and not bad for himself. He either miscalculates the consequences, or decides that it is worthwhile, i.e., better for himself, to incur them.

It is true that most evil-doers would have made different choices had they known in advance what the full consequences of their actions would have been. This is, however, only another way of saying that evil is ignorance.

Ask the criminals who fill our penitentiaries whether or not they did not choose that act which they thought was best for themselves, and whether or not they were mistaken. They tried to choose what was best for them, and because they did not know what was good, they actually made the worst choice possible, through ignorance of what they were really choosing.

The man who steals because he does not expect to be caught and punished would not have stolen had there been a policeman watching him.

In a profounder sense, since that which is good is better than that which is bad, no one could ever choose the bad except through the inadvertent mistake of confusing it with the good.

Man Is Free to Choose The Good

THE PHAEDO, which is one of the literary and dramatic masterpieces of Plato, is an account of the last hours of Socrates, narrated by Phaedo of Elis. It is the most eloquent and profound investigation of the immortality of the soul that can be found in secular literature.

In the brief passage quoted here, Plato offers us the definitive reply to the mechanistic and deterministic points of view, which even today attempt to account for man's behavior as though he were merely a puppet controlled in all his actions and thoughts by the inexorable laws of physics and chemistry and physiological psychology.

(From the "Phaedo")

SOCRATES *Then I heard some one reading, as he said from a book of Anaxagoras, that mind was the disposer and cause of all, and I was delighted at this notion, which appeared quite admirable, and I said to myself: If mind is the disposer, mind will dispose all for the best, and put each particular in the best place; and I argued that if any one desired to find out the cause of the generation of destruction or existence of anything, he must find out what state of being or doing or suffering was best for that thing, and therefore a man had only to consider the best for himself and others, and then he would also know the worse, since the same science comprehended both. And I rejoice to think that I had found in Anaxagoras a teacher of the causes of existence such as I desired, and I imagined that he would tell me first whether the earth is flat or round; and whichever was* true, he would proceed to explain the cause and the necessity of this being so, and then he would teach me the nature of the best and show that this was best; and if he said that the earth was in the center, he would further explain that this position was the best, and I should be satisfied with the explanation given, and not want any other sort of cause.

What expectations I had formed, and how grievously was I disappointed! As I proceeded, I found my philosopher altogether forsaking mind or any other principle of order, but having recourse to air, and ether, and water, and other eccentricities. I might compare him to a person who began by maintaining generally that mind is the cause of the action of Socrates, but who, when he endeavoured to explain the causes of my several actions in detail, went on to show that I sit here because my body is made up of bones and muscles; and the bones, as he would say, are hard and have joints which divide them, and the muscles are elastic, and they cover the bones, which have also a covering or environment of flesh and skin which contains them; and as the bones are lifted at their joints by the contraction or relaxation of the muscles, I am able to bend my limbs, and this is why I am sitting here in a curved posture—that is what he would say; and he would have a similar explanation of my talking to you, which he would attribute to sound, and air, and hearing, and he would assign ten thousand other causes of the same sort, forgetting to mention the true cause, which is, that the Athenians have thought fit to condemn me, and accordingly I have thought it better and more right to remain here and undergo my sentence; for I am inclined to think that these muscles and bones of mine would have gone off long ago to Megara or Boeotia—by the dog they would, if they had been moved only by their own idea of what was best, and if I had not chosen the better and nobler part, instead of playing truant and running away, of enduring any punishment which the state inflicts. There is surely a strange confusion of causes and conditions in all this. It may be said,

ENJOY THE COMPANY OF THREE OF THE WISEST MEN WHO EVER LIVED

(Continued from other side)

The selections themselves are remarkable values. They are carefully printed on expensive paper stock. They are hard-bound in matched sand-colored buckram, worked and stamped in crimson, black, and genuine gold. And through direct-to-the public distribution, we are able to offer our members these deluxe editions for only $3.89 each, plus shipping.

Interested? We will send you the first three selections, Plato, Aristotle and Marcus Aurelius—all three for this special introductory price of $1.00, plus shipping.

We know what charmers these three wise men are. We are betting that you will be so taken by them that you will want to stay in the Club and meet some of your friends, including the greatest story tellers, philosophers, poets and historians the world has ever known.

Do not send any money now. We'll bill you later. Just fill in and mail the attached postage-paid card, today, while you are thinking about it and while the invitation still stands.

THE CLASSICS CLUB
Roslyn, L.I., New York 11576

Please enroll me as a Trial Member, and send me at once the THREE beautiful Classics Club Editions of PLATO, ARISTOTLE AND MARCUS AURELIUS. I enclose NO MONEY IN ADVANCE; within a week after receiving my books, I will either return them and owe nothing, or keep them for the special new-member introductory price of ONLY $1.00 (plus a few cents mailing charges) for ALL OF THESE THREE superb volumes.

As a member, I am to receive advance descriptions of all future selections, but am not obligated to buy any. For each future volume I decide to keep, I will send you only $3.89 (plus a few cents mailing charges). I may reject any volume before or after I receive it, and I may cancel my membership at any time. (Books shipped in U.S.A. only.)

Mr., Mrs., Miss _____ (Please Print Plainly)

Address _____

City _____ State _____ Zip _____

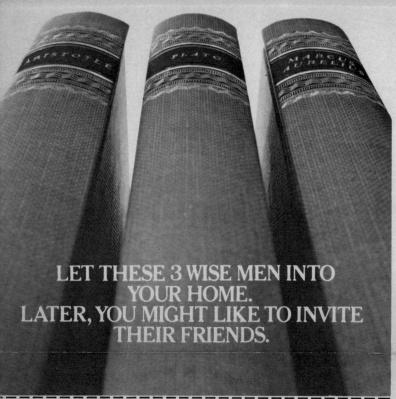

LET THESE 3 WISE MEN INTO
YOUR HOME.
LATER, YOU MIGHT LIKE TO INVITE
THEIR FRIENDS.

Do you have room in your home for three wise men? They are Plato, Aristotle, and Marcus Aurelius . . . three of the wisest, wittiest, most stimulating minds that ever lived.

They still live . . . in the Five Great Dialogues of Plato, the Meditations of Marcus Aurelius, and Aristotle's On Man in the Universe.

All three books (regularly $11.67) can be yours for only $1.00 as your introduction to the Classics Club.

The Classics Club is quite unlike any other book club.

The Club does not offer best sellers that come and go. Instead, it offers its members a chance to stay young through great books that never grow old. These books include Utopia by Thomas More; the complete works of Shakespeare; Benjamin Franklin's Autobiography; Omar Khayyam's Rubaiyat; Walden by Thoreau; and other fresh, spontaneous, even outspoken works that stretch your mind and sweep away the mental cobwebs that hold back most men.

You never have to buy any of these books. (To force you to buy a classic would be barbaric.) As a member, take only those books you really want to own. And, at any time, you may cancel your membership, without penalty or hurt feelings.

(Continued on other side) →

indeed, that without bones and muscles and the other parts of the body I cannot execute my purposes. But to say that I do as I do because of them, and that this is the way in which mind acts, and not from the choice of the best, is a very careless and idle mode of speaking. I wonder that they cannot distinguish the cause from the condition, which the many, feeling about in the dark, are always mistaking and misnaming.

The "Phaedo" is one of the great Platonic, rather than Socratic, dialogues. Plato himself is dominant in these lines, and his contributions are presented in a literary style which is so flawless that it almost overshadows the philosophic excellence of Plato's thinking.

With uncanny prescience in his critical comments on the doctrine of his famous pre-Socratic predecessor, Anaxagoras, Plato anticipates the basic weakness of the arguments used by "mechanists" and "materialists" to this very day.

He discovers that Anaxagoras, whose fame rests on his saying that "mind is the disposer and the cause of all" does not really believe his own teaching, but is actually an advocate of a materialistic, mechanistic doctrine. Plato points out the absurdity of any attempt to account for Socrates refusing to escape from prison because his bones and muscles are governed by mechanical laws. These are merely the "conditions"; that is, the factors in the absence of which the "cause" could not operate. The true cause is that the "Athenians have thought fit to condemn me, and accordingly I have thought it better and more right to remain here and undergo my sentence."

Men are not mere puppets, or stimulus-response machines controlled by the laws of conditioned reflexes and mechanics. Their actions are determined, in the final analysis, by their understanding of the "Idea of the Good," which is the True, and the Beautiful.

Men are free to choose the good, and choose anything else only through ignorance or error.

Socrates remained in prison to face his sentence because his mind controlled his bones and muscles through his will, which was in turn determined by his Idea of the Good.

The Grave Is Not The End of Life

THE GREAT IDEAS pronounced in the "Phaedo," that the soul is immortal, and that the soul is rewarded in heaven for its virtuous conduct on earth, are among the basic philosophic insights or intuitions on which every one of the world's great religions is based, even though not every teacher of religion would agree with Plato that the evil soul cannot be forgiven in heaven without first receiving its just punishment for the evil it has done on earth.

The intuitive knowledge on which Plato's rationalistic idealism rests is in its essence identical with the intuitions on which religious faith is grounded. Thus one cannot be a Platonist without being religious, nor can one be religious without in a sense being a Platonist.

(From the "Phaedo")

SOCRATES *Such is the nature of the other world; and when the dead arrive at the place to which the genius of each severally guides them, first of all, they have sentence passed upon them, as they have lived well and piously or not. And those who appear to have lived neither well nor ill, go to the river Acheron, and embarking in any vessels which they may find, are carried in them to the lake, and there they dwell and are purified of their evil deeds, and having suffered the penalty of the wrongs which they have done to others, they are absolved, and receive the rewards of their good deeds, each of them according to his deserts. But those who appear to be incurable by reason of the greatness of their crimes—who have committed many and terrible deeds of sacrilege, murders foul and violent, or the like —such are hurled into Tartarus which is their suitable destiny, and they never come out.*

soc. *Wherefore,* simmias, *seeing all these things, what ought not we to do that we may obtain virtue and wisdom in this life? Fair is the prize, and the hope great!*

A man of sense ought not to say, nor will I be very confident, that the description which I have given of the soul and her mansions is exactly true. But I do say that, inasmuch as the soul is shown to be immortal, he may venture to think, not improperly or unworthily, that something of the kind is true. The venture is a glorious one, and he ought to comfort himself with words like these, which is the reason why I lengthen out the tale. Wherefore, I say, let a man be of good cheer about his soul, who having cast away the pleasures and ornaments of the body as alien to him and working harm rather than good, has sought after the pleasures of knowledge; and has arrayed the soul, not in some foreign attire, but in her own proper jewels, temperance, and justice, and courage, and nobility, and truth—in these adorned she is ready to go on her journey to the world below, when her hour comes. You, simmias *and* cebes, *and all other men, will depart at some time or other. Me already, as a tragic poet would say, the voice of fate calls. Soon I must drink the poison; and I think that I had better repair to the bath first, in order that the women may not have the trouble of washing my body after I am dead.*

crito *When he had done speaking,* crito *said: And have you any commands for us,* socrates—*anything to say about your children, or any other matter in which we can serve you?*

soc. *Nothing particular,* crito, *he replied: only, as I have always told you, take care of yourselves; that is a service which you may be ever rendering to me and mine and to all of us, whether you promise to do so or not. But if you have no thought for yourselves, and care not to walk according to the rule which I have prescribed for you, not now for the first time, however much you may profess or promise at the moment, it will be of no avail.*

crito *We will do our best, said* crito: *And in what way shall we bury you?*

soc. *In any way that you like; but you must get hold of me, and take care that I do not run away from you.* Then he turned to us, and added with a smile:—*I cannot make Crito believe that I am the same Socrates who have been talking and conducting the argument; he fancies that I am the other Socrates whom he will soon see, a dead body—and he asks, How shall he bury me? And though I have spoken many words in the endeavour to show that when I have drunk the poison I shall leave you and go to the joys of the blessed,—these words of mine, with which I was comforting you and myself, have had, as I perceive, no effect upon Crito. And therefore I want you to be surety for me to him now, as at the trial he was surety to the judges for me: but let the promise be of another sort; for he was surety for me to the judges that I would remain, and you must be my surety to him that I shall not remain, but go away and depart; and then he will suffer less at my death, and not be grieved when he sees my body being burned or buried. I would not have him sorrow at my hard lot, or say at the burial, Thus we lay out Socrates, or, Thus we follow him to the grave or bury him; for false words are not only evil in themselves, but they infect the soul with evil. Be of good cheer then, my dear* CRITO, *and say that you are burying my body only, and do with that whatever is usual, and what you think best.*

The Socratic-Platonic philosophy can be designated, in technical terms, as an *idealistic* or *rationalistic* philosophy.

Idealism is the doctrine that affirms that the highest, truest and most genuine form of reality is the "idea," and that ideas alone are fully real.

Metaphysics is that branch of philosophy which asks questions like these: "What is truly real?" "What is the innermost essence of all reality?" or "Which is more real, a thing or an idea, a body or a mind, the natural world or the spiritual world?"

Idealism, then, is one of the answers to these questions of metaphysics. The doctrine of idealism, namely, that "ideas alone are genuinely real," is itself an idea, and this idea is believed by all true disciples of Socrates and Plato to be perhaps the greatest idea in the history of the world's great ideas.

Rationalism, which is derived from the word which means "reason" (in the sense of reasoning power) is one of the possible methods of acquiring knowledge.

Knowledge comes to us either (a) directly through our senses or (b) indirectly through our reasoning powers, or (c) immediately and directly through the intuitive powers of our minds.

Reasoning is the process whereby we are able to know that certain ideas or assertions "imply" or "entail" the truth of other ideas or assertions.

Certain ideas are connected to each other in such a way that if the first one is true, the second one must be true. This can be expressed by the formula, if "a" is true, then "b" is true, where "a" and "b" are ideas or assertions.

For example, the idea "man" implies the idea "mortality." We can assert, therefore, that if Mr. B is a man, then Mr. B is a mortal; or if Mr. B is a man, then Mr. B will die some day.

If we actually witness the death of Mr. B with our own eyes, then we have learned empirically, or through our senses and directly, that Mr. B was a mortal. This method of gaining knowledge through our senses is known as the method of empiricism.

If we reach the conclusion that Mr. B is a mortal by arguing that if he is a man, he must be mortal, then we have gained our knowledge rationally and indirectly, through our mental powers. This method of gaining knowledge is called the method of rationalism.

Archimedes, who invented the lever, was able to say: "Give me a fixed and immovable point on which to rest my lever and I can move the world."

In much the same way the rationalist is able to say: "Give me an idea which is so true that it can never be doubted, and I can use it as the foundation of a whole system of philosophy in which every assertion is just as true as the foundation premise. (Once we know that A is true, then we know that B must be true. If B is true, then C is true, if C is true, then D is true, and so on through the entire system.)

But how can we ever know that A is true in the first place? There's the rub. We cannot learn it by reasoning, any more than we can pull ourselves up by our own bootstraps. All we can do by reasoning is to learn that *if our first assertion is true,* then all the implications, which follow from it according to the laws of valid reasoning, must also be true. But the laws of reasoning are silent concerning the truth of the crucial first premise.

In order to establish the truth of the first premise of a rational system, we must employ one of two other methods of knowing, either empiricism, or intuitionism.

The method of empiricism, as was mentioned earlier, accepts the report of the senses as final. The idea which we call empiricism, is another of the great ideas in the history of world thought. It has been expressed precisely and delicately in a fragment of oriental verse:

> *Whether the fruit be bitter*
> *Or whether it be sweet,*
> *The first bite tells.**

But knowledge acquired by the method of empiricism is limited to the particular case, here and now. What is true of the particular case, can be proven only by empirical evidence, that is, the testimony of the senses.

This testimony or proof cannot by itself throw any light on future cases which have not been observed and proven yet. Nor can it ever demonstrate any truth which must hold for all possible cases.

For example, we can draw any number of lines we wish between two points, P_1 and P_2, and measure their lengths, and prove by actual empirical measurement that the line which is the straightest is the shortest.

One of the axioms of plane Euclidean geometry, how-

---

* A. Waley, *Japanese Poetry. The Uta.* (Clarendon Press.)

ever, which are held to be true for *all possible cases*, informs us that a straight line is the shortest distance between two points. How do we know this?

Certain ideas are so clear and so simple that when we encounter them we know directly and immediately without needing any proof whatsoever that they are indeed true. Technically this method of knowing is called the method of intuition.

Thus the process or method of intuition may be defined as the process of knowing or apprehending self-evident truths, directly and immediately, without the necessity for any external proof whatsoever.

This method is very important, not only for establishing the foundations of mathematics, but those of philosophy and religion as well.

All the teachings of Socrates, and the writings of Plato, rest on intuitive knowledge.

The real, the true, the good, the beautiful, how do we know what they are? We recognize them intuitively, How do we know that a sunset or a symphony is beautiful? We just know. We know immediately, and directly, and without proof.

Of course, we see the sunset through our eyes, and we hear the symphony through our ears, but we know that they are beautiful by the intuitive power of our minds.

Then how do we know that some acts are good and others are bad? Again the answer is the same, by intuition.

It is intuition that tells us that God exists and rules the world with love and justice; that the soul is immortal and is rewarded or punished in the hereafter according to the degree of virtue it achieves in this world.

Thus we have seen some of the ways man has of learning about the world in which he lives.

Actually, none of the methods of knowing is pure and exclusive, each one involves all the others, but in each case one method is more dominant than the others, and receives the most emphasis.

At the heart of the rationalistic idealism of Socrates and Plato is a sincere religious faith. Great scientists

are usually religious men. In the Platonic system, the
existence of God and the immortality of the soul, together with the doctrine of reward or punishment in
the hereafter, are accepted as intuitively certain truths.
It is only through intuition that these fundamental truths
can be established.

Should an Unjust Law Be Obeyed?

AFTER SOCRATES has been condemned to die, his friends, with the assistance and approval of his jailers, make arrangements for him to escape on the night before he was to be executed. Crito comes to Socrates to deliver him from prison, and Socrates explains to him why he cannot run away.

(From the "Crito")

SOCRATES *Then I will go on to the next point, which may be put in the form of a question: Ought a man to do what he admits to be right, or ought he to betray the right?*
CRITO *He ought to do what he thinks right.*
SOC. *But if this is true, what is the application? In leaving the prison against the will of the Athenians, do I wrong any? or rather do I not wrong those whom I ought least to wrong? Do I not desert the principles which were acknowledged by us to be just—what do you say?*
CR. *I cannot tell, SOCRATES; for I do not know.*
SOC. *Then consider the matter in this way:—Imagine that I am about to play truant (you may call the proceeding by any name which you like), and the laws and the government come and interrogate me: 'Tell us, Socrates,' they say; 'what are you about? are you not going by an act of yours to overturn us—the laws, and the whole state, as far as in you lies? Do you imagine that a state can subsist and not be overthrown, in which the decisions of law have no power, but are set aside and trampled upon by individuals?'*

SOC. *'Tell us—What complaint have you to make against us which justifies you in attempting to destroy us and the state? In the first place did we not bring you into*

existence? Your father married your mother by our aid
and begat you. Say whether you have any objection to
urge against those of us who regulate marriage?' None,
I should reply. 'Or against those of us who after birth
regulate the nurture and education of children, in which
you also were trained? Were not the laws, which have
the charge of education, right in commanding your
father to train you in music and gymnastic?' Right, I
should reply. 'Well then, since you were brought into
the world and nurtured and educated by us, can you
deny in the first place that you are our child and slave,
as your fathers were before you? And if this is true you
are not on equal terms with us; nor can you think that
you have a right to do to us what we are doing to you.
Would you have any right to strike or revile or do any
other evil to your father or your master, if you had one,
because you have been struck or reviled by him, or received some other evil at his hands?—you would not say
this? And because we think right to destroy you, do you
think that you have any right to destroy us in return,
and your country as far as in you lies? Will you, O pro-
fessor of true virtue, pretend that you are justified in
this? Has a philosopher like you failed to discover that
our country is more to be valued and higher and holier
far than mother or father or any ancestor, and more to
be regarded in the eyes of the gods and of men of understanding? also to be soothed, and gently and rever-
ently entreated when angry, even more than a father,
and either to be persuaded, or if not persuaded, to be
obeyed? And when we are punished by her, whether
with imprisonment or stripes, the punishment is to be
endured in silence; and if she lead us to wounds or
death in battle, thither we follow as is right; neither may
any one yield or retreat or leave his rank, but whether
in battle or in a court of law, or in any other place, he
must do what his city and his country order him; or he
must change their view of what is just: and if he may do
no violence to his father or mother, much less may he do
violence to his country.' What answer shall we make to
this, CRITO? Do the laws speak truly, or do they not?

CR. *I think that they do.*

SOC. *Then will they not say:* 'You, Socrates, are breaking the covenants and agreements which you made with us at your leisure, not in any haste or under any compulsion or deception, but after you have had seventy years to think of them, during which time you were at liberty to leave the city, if we were not to your mind, or if our covenants appeared to you to be unfair. You had your choice, and might have gone either to Lacedaemon or Crete, both which states are often praised by you for their good government, or to some other Hellenic or foreign state. Whereas you, above all other Athenians, seemed to be so fond of the state, or, in other words, of us her laws (and who would care about a state which has no laws?), that you never stirred out of her; the halt, the blind, the maimed were not more stationary in her than you were. And now you run away and forsake your agreements. Not so, Socrates, if you will take our advice; do not make yourself ridiculous by escaping out of the city.'

SOC. 'Listen, then, Socrates, to us who have brought you up. Think not of life and children first, and of justice afterwards, but of justice first, that you may be justified before the princes of the world below. For neither will you nor any that belong to you be happier or holier or juster in this life, or happier in another, if you do as Crito bids. Now you depart in innocence, a sufferer and not a doer of evil; a victim, not of the laws but of men. But if you go forth, returning evil for evil, and injury for injury, breaking the covenants and agreements which you have made with us, and wronging those whom you ought least of all to wrong, that is to say, yourself, your friends, your country, and us, we shall be angry with you while you live, and our brethren, the laws in the world below, will receive you as an enemy; for they will know that you have done your best to destroy us. Listen, then, to us and not to Crito.' *This, dear* CRITO, *is the voice which I seem to hear murmuring in my ears, like the*

*sound of the flute in the ears of the mystic; that voice, I
say, is humming in my ears, and prevents me from hearing any other. And I know that anything more which you
may say will be vain. Yet speak, if you have anything to
say.*

CR. *I have nothing to say,* SOCRATES.

SOC. *Leave me then,* CRITO, *to fulfill the will of God, and
to follow whither he leads.*

Laws are administered by men. And since men are not
infallible, they can arrive at unjust verdicts even under
the wisest and best laws.

One of the basic principles of living in a democracy is
that no individual can set himself above the verdicts of
the law, even if the verdict in a single case is an unjust
one.

Socrates, who was playing a bigger game than baseball,
was called "out" by the umpire. It was a bad call, and
everyone knew it. Socrates' friends were indignant. They
urged him to refuse to accept the umpire's decision and
to leave the game.

But Socrates knew that if he refused to abide by the
decision and walked off the field, he would not only break
up and lose the game, but he would be undoing his life's
work. He would be helping to destroy the profound respect and love for justice which he had tried to instill in
his fellow citizens by his own example of a lifetime of
dedication to the great ideas by which he had always
lived.

Socrates had spent his entire life in the search for the
true, the good, the beautiful, and the just. He had learned
from his investigations that as far as justice is concerned,
we cannot find it exemplified in the fate of an individual.
Instead, we must look for it in the workings of a democratic state which strives to provide justice for all through
its laws, even though it may not succeed in every single
case.

Socrates was aware that in a democracy, it was possible
for a bad law to get on the books, or for a judge to make
a mistake, or even to be incompetent or dishonest. But he
was clearminded enough to recognize that this did not
make the *system of democracy* wrong. In a democracy, if

a law is a bad one, the lawmakers can change it by due process. If a judge proves to be incompetent or dishonest, he can be impeached and replaced.

But while the law is on the books, and the judge is on the bench, the law must be obeyed and the judge's verdicts carried out. Only a higher court can set aside a judge's verdict, and then only on the basis of the law under which the previous judge atttempted to interpret and dispense justice. No citizen can set aside either the law or a judge's decision under that law.

Socrates knew that a democratic state could not be perfect. But he was convinced that in the long run and in actual practice it comes closer to providing justice for all than any other kind of government would.

He did not want his friends and his fellow citizens to lose their faith in democracy—he knew that they would not find it easy to understand why so wise and just a person as Socrates had to suffer an injustice at the hands of the law when he could have easily escaped if he had wanted to.

By freely giving up his chance to escape, and sacrificing his life to preserve the democratic system of justice to which he was dedicated, Socrates knew that neither his friends, nor the citizens of Athens, nor the world would ever forget his final "lecture" on democracy.

Man Is The Measure of All Things

THE GREATEST of all the Sophists, except Socrates himself, was Protagoras. In this dialogue, which is acknowledged as one of Plato's greatest literary masterpieces, the ideas of Protagoras are presented so brilliantly by Plato, that to this day, they gain disciples for a point of view diametrically opposed to Plato's own. Protagoras is the patron saint of contemporary empiricism, the method of acquiring knowledge which places primary emphasis upon the knowledge which comes to us through our senses. Protagoras' famous doctrine of relativism summed up in his teaching: "Man is the measure of all things," is one of the great ideas of all time.

(From the "Protagoras")

SOCRATES *Protagoras ended, and in my ear*

> 'So charming left his voice, that I the while
> Thought him still speaking; still stood fixed
>   to hear.' *

At length, when the truth dawned upon me, that he had really finished, not without difficulty I began to collect myself, and looking at Hippocrates, I said to him: O son of Apollodorus, how deeply grateful I am to you for having brought me hither; I would not have missed the speech of Protagoras for a great deal. For I used to imagine that no human care could make men good; but I know better now. Yet I have still one very small difficulty which I am sure that Protagoras will easily explain, as he has already explained so much. If a man were to go and consult Pericles or any of our great

---

* Borrowed by Milton, *Paradise Lost*, viii. 2, 3.

speakers about these matters, he might perhaps hear as fine a discourse; but then when one has a question to ask of any of them, like books, they can neither answer nor ask; and if any one challenges the least particular of their speech, they go ringing on in a long harangue, like brazen pots, which when they are struck continue to sound unless some one put his hand upon them; whereas our friend Protagoras can not only make a good speech, as he has already shown, but when he is asked a question he can answer briefly; and when he asks he will wait and hear the answer; and this is a very rare gift. Now I, PROTAGORAS, want to ask of you a little question, which if you will only answer, I shall be quite satisfied. You were saying that virtue can be taught;— that I will take upon your authority, and there is no one to whom I am more ready to trust. But I marvel at one thing about which I should like to have my mind set at rest. You were speaking of Zeus sending justice and reverence to men; and several times while you were speaking, justice, and temperance, and holiness, and all these qualities, were described by you as if together they made up virtue. Now I want you to tell me truly whether virtue is one whole, of which justice and temperance and holiness are parts; or whether all these are only the names of one and the same thing: that is the doubt which still lingers in my mind.

PROTAGORAS *There is no difficulty, SOCRATES, in answering that the qualities of which you are speaking are the parts of virtue which is one.*

SOC. *And are they parts, I said, in the same sense in which mouth, nose, and eyes, and ears, are the parts of a face; or are they like the parts of gold, which differ from the whole and from one another only in being larger or smaller?*

PROT. *I should say that they differed, SOCRATES, in the first way; they are related to one another as the parts of a face are related to the whole face.*

SOC. *And do men have some one part and some another part of virtue? Or if a man has one part, must he also have all the others?*

soc. *If what you say is true, then the argument is absurd which affirms that a man often does evil knowingly, when he might abstain, because he is seduced and overpowered by pleasure; or again; when you say that a man knowingly refuses to do what is good because he is overcome at the moment by pleasure. And that this is ridiculous will be evident if only we give up the use of various names, such as pleasant and painful, and good and evil. As there are two things, let us call them by two names—first, good and evil, and then pleasant and painful. Assuming this, let us go on to say that a man does evil knowing that he does evil. But some one will ask, Why? Because he is overcome, is the first answer. And by what is he overcome? the inquirer will proceed to ask. And we shall not be able to reply 'By pleasure,' for the name of pleasure has been exchanged for that of good. In our answer, then, we shall only say that he is overcome. 'By what?' he will reiterate. By the good, we shall have to reply; indeed we shall. Nay, but our questioner will rejoin with a laugh, if he be one of the swaggering sort, 'That is too ridiculous, that a man should do what he knows to be evil when he ought not, because he is overcome by good. Is that,' he will ask, 'because the good was worthy or not worthy of conquering the evil?' And in answer to that we shall clearly reply, Because it was not worthy; for if it had been worthy, then he who, as we say, was overcome by pleasure, would not have been wrong. 'But how,' he will reply, 'can the good be unworthy of the evil, or the evil of the good?' Is not the real explanation that they are out of proportion to one another, either as greater and smaller, or more and fewer? This we cannot deny. And when you speak of being overcome—'what do you mean,' he will say, 'but that you choose the greater evil in exchange for the lesser good?' Admitted. And now substitute the names of pleasure and pain for good and evil, and say, not as before, that a man does what is evil knowingly, but that he does what is painful knowingly, and because he is overcome by pleasure, which is unworthy to overcome. What measure is there of the relations of pleasure to* pain other than excess and defect, which means that they become greater and smaller, and more and fewer, and differ in degree? For if any one says: 'Yes, Socrates, but immediate pleasure differs widely from future pleasure and pain'—To that I should reply: And do they differ in anything but in pleasure and pain? There can be no other measure of them. And do you, like a skillful weigher, put into the balance the pleasures and the pains, and their nearness and distance, and weigh them, and then say which outweighs the other. If you weigh pleasures against pleasures, you of course take the more and greater; or if you weigh pains against pains, then you choose that course of action in which the painful is exceeded by the pleasant, whether the distant by the near or the near by the distant; and you avoid that course of action in which the pleasant is exceeded by the painful. Would you not admit, my friends, that this is true?

SOC. Now suppose happiness to consist in doing or choosing the greater, and in not doing or in avoiding the less, what would be the saving principle of human life? Would not the art of measuring be the saving principle; or would the power of appearance? Is not the latter that deceiving art which makes us wander up and down and take the things at one time of which we repent at another, both in our actions and in our choice of things great and small? But the art of measurement would do away with the effect of appearances, and, showing the truth, would fain teach the soul at last to find rest in the truth, and would thus save our life. Would not mankind generally acknowledge that the art which accomplishes this result is the art of measurement?
PROT. Yes, he said, the art of measurement.
SOC. Suppose, again, the salvation of human life to depend on the choice of odd and even, and on the knowledge of when a man ought to choose the greater or less, either in reference to themselves or to each other, and whether near or at a distance; what would be the saving principle of our lives? Would not knowledge?—a knowledge of measuring, when the question is one of excess and defect. . . .

soc. *Then, my friends, what do you say to this? Are not all actions honourable and useful, of which the tendency is to make life painless and pleasant? The honourable work is also useful and good?*

This was admitted.

Then, I said, if the pleasant is the good, nobody does anything under the idea or conviction that some other thing would be better and is also attainable, when he might do the better. And this inferiority of a man to himself is merely ignorance, as the superiority of a man to himself is wisdom.

They all assented.

And is not ignorance the having a false opinion and being deceived about important matters?

To this also they unanimously assented.

Then, I said, no man voluntarily pursues evil, or that which he thinks to be evil. To prefer evil to good is not in human nature; and when a man is compelled to choose one of two evils, no one will choose the greater when he may have the less.

Here, in the selection from the "Protagoras," we have one of the few positive teachings of Socrates.

The "Protagoras" is one of the four great masterpieces of literature and philosophy in which the ideas of Plato rather than Socrates are most significant.

Socrates has already taught that all wrong-doing is involuntary, and that the virtues are one.

In the "Protagoras," Plato starts with the relatively simple ethical precept of Socrates, but he manages to develop the implication of the precept with a skill that goes far beyond that of his teacher.

Protagoras attempts to demonstrate that a man often does evil knowingly when he might abstain, because he is seduced and overpowered by pleasure; or again when you say that a man refuses knowingly to do what is good because he is overcome at the moment by pleasure.

But if pleasure is the good, then the argument becomes manifestly absurd, since it affirms for all practical purposes that to do evil knowingly is equivalent to being overcome by good. There are obviously only two alternatives:

(a) Either pleasure is not the good, but we think it is when we choose it instead of the good, in which case we have made the wrong choice through ignorance or error;

(b) If, for the sake of argument, pleasure were the good, we could never voluntarily choose anything else in preference to it, unless we mistake a lesser quantity of good or pleasure for a greater quantity of good or pleasure. That is to say, any one who is able to make a free and unrestricted choice between two pleasures or goods, one lesser and one greater, would never choose the lesser, except by mistake in measurement.

Once more we are driven to the same conclusion, any-one who fails to choose the good, would do so because of a mistake in measurement, or in ignorance.

The little boy who eats too many green apples, which is a very pleasant activity, has failed to calculate the severity of the bellyache which follows. Had he been able to contemplate the excruciating pains of the belly-ache, he would never have eaten the apples, as his ab-horrence of green apples forever after proves.

The critical importance of the problem posed by Soc-rates, "can virtue be taught?" and his definitive reply that all wrong-doing is only miscalculation, since to know the good is to choose it, is the basis for our most enlightened present-day programs for the rehabilitation of criminals. From this point of view, criminals are not so much bad as ignorant. They do not need to be pun-ished; they need to be educated.

While it is true that there are habitual criminals who do not respond, the most enlightened work of present-day parole boards is that which is based on these prin-ciples.

If the desirability of one quantity of pleasure is weighed against the desirability of another quantity of pleasure, no one who knows how to measure them correctly would fail to choose the greater; and a similar statement could be made about the avoidance of a greater or lesser pain.

Plato and Protagoras represent opposite poles of thought. For Plato there is an absolute goodness, truth and beauty whose values are not affected by what we or anyone (even God himself) thinks or does about them. For Protagoras, absolute values are nonsense. Real values are practical values, as determined by criteria set by man himself. In short, as things appear to man, so they are.

How Knowledge Is Possible

Theaetetus, who, like Socrates, was snub-nosed, homely and very brilliant, while a young man at the time of the dialogue, later became a member of Plato's academy, studied philosophy and mathematics under Plato and became one of the greatest mathematicians of his day.

The "Theaetetus" is concerned with one of the most abstruse problems of philosophy, namely, what is knowledge. This is the central problem of that branch of philosophy known as epistemology. In this dialogue, Plato anticipates most of the solutions which have since been advanced.

(From the "Theaetetus")

SOCRATES *I would have you imagine, then, that there exists in the mind of man a block of wax, which is of different sizes in different men; harder, moister, and having more or less of purity in one than another, and in some of an intermediate quality.*

THEAETETUS *I see.*

SOC. *Let us say that this tablet is a gift of Memory, the mother of the Muses; and that when we wish to remember anything which we have seen, or heard, or thought in our own minds, we hold the wax to the perceptions and thoughts, and in that material receive the impression of them as from the seal of a ring; and that we remember and know what is imprinted as long as the image lasts; but when the image is effaced, or cannot be taken, then we forget and do not know.*

THEAET. *Very good.*

SOC. *Now, when a person has this knowledge, and is considering something which he sees or hears, may not false opinion arise in the following manner?*

THEAET. *In what manner?*

soc. *When he thinks what he knows, sometimes to be what he knows, and sometimes to be what he does not know. We were wrong before in denying the possibility of this.*

THEAET. *And how would you amend the former statement?*

soc. *I should begin by making a list of the impossible cases which must be excluded. (1) No one can think one thing to be another when he does not perceive either of them, but has the memorial or seal of both of them in his mind; nor can any mistaking of one thing for another occur, when he only knows one, and does not know, and has no impression of the other; nor can he think that one thing which he does not know is another thing which he does not know, or that what he does not know is what he knows; nor (2) that one thing which he perceives is another thing which he perceives, or that something which he perceives is something which he does not perceive; or that something which he does not perceive is something else which he does not perceive; or that something which he does not perceive is something which he perceives. . . .*

soc. *The only possibility of erroneous opinion is, when knowing you and Theodorus, and having on the waxen block the impression of both of you given as by a seal, but seeing you imperfectly and at a distance, I try to assign the right impression of memory to the right visual impression, and to fit this into its own print: if I succeed, recognition will take place; but if I fail and transpose them, putting the foot into the wrong shoe—that is to say, putting the vision of either of you on to the wrong impression, or if my mind, like the sight in a mirror, which is transferred from right to left, err by reason of some similar affection, then 'heterodoxy' and false opinion ensues.*

THEAET. *Yes, SOCRATES, you have described the nature of opinion with wonderful exactness.*

soc. *And the origin of truth and error is as follows:— When the wax in the soul of any one is deep and abun-*

*dant, and smooth and perfectly tempered, then the im-
pressions which pass through the senses and sink into
the heart of the soul, as Homer says in a parable, meaning to indicate the likeness of the soul to wax; these, I
say, being pure and clear, and having a sufficient depth
of wax, are also lasting, and minds, such as these, easily
learn and easily retain, and are not liable to confusion,
but have true thoughts, for they have plenty of room,
and having clear impressions of things, as we term them,
quickly distribute them into their proper places on the
block. And such men are called wise. Do you agree?*

One of the subdivisions of philosophy is technically
termed *epistemology*, or the theory of knowledge. This
term is derived from the Greek word "epistemos," meaning knowledge, and "logos," meaning discourse on.
Epistemology is concerned with the nature, the limits,
and the validity of human knowledge. One of the basic
treatises in the field of epistemology is "The Theaetetus"
of Plato. Here he anticipates the later developments in
this field which were made by the noted British empirical
philosopher, John Locke, whose famous *Essay Concerning Human Understanding* was published in 1690.

The basic premise of Locke's system of epistemology
was his teaching that, at birth, the mind is a *tabula rasa*,
a blank tablet, on which experience writes all of our
knowledge.

Locke prided himself on being a hard-headed man of
common sense, and on his rejection of any knowledge
that did not come from experience.

But as he developed, with rigorous logic, the implications of his starting postulate, he became enmeshed
in sorely perplexing difficulties that demonstrated the
inadequacy of his first principle. Had he been a better
student of Plato, he could have learned from the *Theaetetus* that the wax-tablet theory is inadequate to explain
error.

The wax-tablet theory accounts very well for successful learning, and to some extent for vague or confused
memories as the wax becomes blurred with age. But as

Plato points out, with exhaustive exactness in the citation quoted, there are several other types of mistakes of memory and knowledge which a good theory of knowledge must account for if it is to be successful.

The Mind Is Not a Wax Tablet

IN THE PREVIOUS CITATION, Plato has persuaded his hearers of the plausibility of his proposal to compare memory to a block of wax upon which experience is impressed. The dialogue continues with a swift and devastating change of mood, and here Plato demolishes his own wax-tablet theory by pointing out that it could never possibly account for error.

(From the "Theaetetus")

SOCRATES *Alas, THEAETETUS, what a tiresome creature is a man who is fond of talking!*

THEAETETUS *What makes you say so?*

SOC. *Because I am disheartened at my own stupidity and tiresome garrulity. . . .*

THEAET. *But what puts you out of heart?*

SOC. *I am not only out of heart, but in positive despair; for I do not know what to answer if any one were to ask me:—O Socrates, have you indeed discovered that false opinion arises neither in the comparison of perceptions with one another nor yet in thought, but in the union of thought and perception? Yes, I shall say, with the complacence of one who thinks that he has made a noble discovery.*

THEAET. *I see no reason why we should be ashamed of our demonstration, SOCRATES.*

SOC. *He will say: You mean to argue that the man whom we only think of and do not see, cannot be confused with the horse which we do not see or touch, but only think of and do not perceive? That I believe to be my meaning, I shall reply.*

THEAET. *Quite right.*

SOC. *Well, then, he will say, according to that argument, the number eleven, which is only thought, can never be mistaken for twelve, which is only thought: How would you answer him?*

THEAET. *I should say that a mistake may very likely arise between the eleven or twelve which are seen or handled, but that no similar mistake can arise between the eleven and twelve which are in the mind.*

SOC. *Well, but do you think that no one ever put before his own mind five and seven,—I do not mean five or seven men or horses, but five or seven in the abstract, which, as we say, are recorded on the waxen block; and in which false opinion is held to be impossible;—did no man ever ask himself how many these numbers make when added together, and answer that they are eleven, while another thinks that they are twelve, or would all agree in thinking and saying that they are twelve?*

THEAET. *Certainly not; many would think that they are eleven, and in the higher numbers the chance of error is greater still; for I assume you to be speaking of numbers in general.*

SOC. *Exactly; and I want you to consider whether this does not imply that the twelve in the waxen block are supposed to be eleven?*

THEAET. *Yes, that seems to be the case.*

SOC. *Then do we not come back to the old difficulty? For he who makes such a mistake does think one thing which he knows to be another thing which he knows; but this, as we said, was impossible. . . .*

SOC. *But, as we are at our wits' end, suppose that we do a shameless thing?*

THEAET. *What is it?*

SOC. *Let us attempt to explain the verb 'to know.'*

THEAET. *And why should that be shameless?*

SOC. *You seem not to be aware that the whole of our discussion from the very beginning has been a search after knowledge, of which we are assumed not to know the nature.*

THEAET. *Nay, but I am well aware.*

SOC. *And is it not shameless when we do not know what knowledge is, to be explaining the verb 'to know'? The truth is,* THEAETETUS, *that we have long been infected with logical impurity. Thousands of times have we repeated the words 'we know,' and 'do not know,' and 'we have or have not science or knowledge,' as if we could understand what we are saying to one another, so long as we remain ignorant about knowledge; and at this moment we are using the words 'we understand,' 'we are ignorant,' as though we could still employ them when deprived of knowledge or science.*

The superior philosophical acumen of Plato, as compared to the more naive thinking of John Locke, is evidenced in Plato's quick rejection of the wax-tablet theory because of its obvious failure to account for various types of error, and his turning instead to the re-examination of the meaning of the verb "to know."

By his sophisticated reflection of the knowing process back upon itself, by pointing out the necessity of checking and probing and re-examining the structure of the knowing process itself, Plato created one of the most abstruse and one of the most important branches of philosophy.

The importance of epistemology for science as well as philosophy is just becoming recognized today. It has been said by Eddington, one of the great mathematical physicists of our day, that modern physics has gone just about as far as it can go unless physics first makes new advances in epistemology.

Epistemology is one of the most forbidding and difficult areas of philosophical investigation, and requires of its students a sustained enthusiasm in the search for wisdom to carry them through its abstract flights.

Some of the greatest contributions to philosophy have been made in this field, particularly by David Hume and Immanuel Kant, on whose epistemological studies the logical structure of modern science can be said to rest.

An Idea Is Like a Bird In a Cage

HERE PLATO PRESENTS the brilliant figure of the Aviary
—which he offers in half-seriousness as a speculative hypothesis in place of the wax-tablet theory which he has
rejected. It affords an arresting introduction to the basic
problems of epistemology.

(From the "Theaetetus")

SOCRATES   *But, seeing that we are no great wits, shall
I venture to say what knowing is? for I think that the
attempt may be worth making.*
THEAETETUS   *Then by all means venture, and no one
shall find fault with you for using the forbidden terms.*
SOC.   *You have heard the common explanation of the
verb 'to know'?*
THEAET.   *I think so, but I do not remember it at the
moment.*
SOC.   *They explain the word 'to know' as meaning 'to
have knowledge.'*
THEAET.   *True.*
SOC.   *I should like to make a slight change, and say 'to
possess' knowledge.*
THEAET.   *How do the two expressions differ?*
SOC.   *Perhaps there may be no difference; but still I
should like you to hear my view, that you may help
me to test it.*
THEAET.   *I will, if I can.*
SOC.   *I should distinguish 'having' from 'possessing': for
example, a man may buy and keep under his control a
garment which he does not wear; and then we should
say, not that he has, but that he possesses the garment.*
THEAET.   *It would be the correct expression.*
SOC.   *Well, may not a man 'possess' and yet not 'have'
knowledge in the sense of which I am speaking? As you
may suppose a man to have caught wild birds—doves or*

93

*any other birds—and to be keeping them in an aviary
which he has constructed at home; we might say of him
in one sense, that he always has them because he possesses them, might we not?*

THEAET. *Yes.*

SOC. *And yet, in another sense, he has none of them;
but they are in his power, and he has got them under
his hand in an enclosure of his own, and can take and
have them whenever he likes;—he can catch any which
he likes, and let the bird go again, and he may do so as
often as he pleases.*

THEAET. *True.*

SOC. *Once more, then, as in what preceded we made a
sort of waxen figment in the mind, so let us now suppose that in the mind of each man there is an aviary of
all sorts of birds—some flocking together apart from the
rest, others in small groups, others solitary, flying any-
where and everywhere.*

THEAET. *Let us imagine such an aviary—and what is to
follow?*

SOC. *We may suppose that the birds are kinds of knowledge, and that when we were children, this receptacle
was empty; whenever a man has gotten and detained in
the enclosure a kind of knowledge, he may be said to
have learned or discovered the thing which is the subject of the knowledge: and this is to know.*

THEAET. *Granted.*

SOC. *And further, when any one wishes to catch any of
these knowledges or sciences, and having taken, to hold
it, and again to let them go, how will he express himself?—will he describe the 'catching' of them and the
original 'possession' in the same words?*

The figure of the aviary with which Plato replaces the
wax-tablet hypothesis, is not only more charming from
a literary point of view, but very much more adequate
philosophically, at least in accounting for error.

If by "having" knowledge is meant writing it firmly
on a wax tablet, it is obviously impossible to explain
how we could ever "read" it incorrectly when we try to

remember it, but if by "having" knowledge we mean "possessing" knowledge in the same way that we possess a number of wild birds that we have captured and put into a bird cage, then it is quite obvious that we could reach into the cage for one bird and pull out another by mistake.

By considering mind and memory to be a dynamic process rather than a static and relatively permanent substance, Plato makes a significant advance in his analysis. This is true despite the fact that while the aviary theory does account remarkably well for error, it can hardly be said to do so for correct knowledge.

The difficulty in this regard is that it blames the birds for flying away rather than the keeper for failing to recapture them. That some ideas are harder to remember than others is not so much a quality of the ideas as the quality of the mind which is learning them. Therefore a mind that learns well would be represented by a bird-keeper who has completely tamed his collection, so that the right bird flies to his shoulder when he calls its name.

But in order to account for error, the birds must remain wild.

We are accordingly left with a paradox that in order to account for error, the birds must be wild; but in order to account for correct knowledge, the birds must be tame—and they cannot be both.

Even if the paradox is resolved by the admission that some birds can be partly trained, the difficulty of blaming the birds for flying away rather than the bird-keeper for failing to recapture them still remains.

It would be a serious mistake, however, to take the figure of the aviary as a hypothesis proposed by Plato as a sober, literal, scientific truth. Instead, it is sheer poetry—and it offers to us, if not a solution of the problems of epistemology, at least an intuitive insight as to what the problems are.

The Nature of "Being" or "Isness"

WHEN SOCRATES was still a young man, Parmenides, who has his own place in the history of the world's great philosophers, was an old man at the zenith of his powers and wisdom. In this dialogue, Plato draws for us the rare picture of the young and rather brash Socrates receiving a lesson in logic from one of the great masters. The dialogue is actually a vehicle for presenting Plato's own contribution to philosophy, his doctrine of Forms or Platonic Ideas, and one of the most abstruse of all of Plato's writings.

(From the "Parmenides")

PARMENIDES SOCRATES, *he said, I admire the bent of your mind towards philosophy; tell me now, was this your own distinction between ideas in themselves and the things which partake of them? and do you think that there is an idea of likeness apart from the likeness which we possess, and of the one and many, and of the other things which Zeno mentioned?*

SOCRATES *I think that there are such ideas, said Socrates.*

PAR. *Parmenides proceeded: And would you also make absolute ideas of the just and the beautiful and the good, and of all that class?*

SOC. *Yes, he said, I should.*

PAR. *And would you make an idea of man apart from us and from all other human creatures, or of fire and water?*

SOC. *I am often undecided, PARMENIDES, as to whether I ought to include them or not.*

PAR. *And would you feel equally undecided, SOCRATES, about things of which the mention may provoke a smile? —I mean such things as hair, mud, dirt, or anything else which is vile and paltry; would you suppose that each*

*of these has an idea distinct from the actual objects with
which we come into contact, or not?*

SOC. *Certainly not, said Socrates; visible things like these
are such as they appear to us, and I am afraid that there
would be an absurdity in assuming any idea of them,
although I sometimes get disturbed, and begin to think
that there is nothing without an idea; but then again,
when I have taken up this position, I run away, because
I am afraid that I may fall into a bottomless pit of nonsense, and perish; and so I return to the ideas of which I
was just now speaking, and occupy myself with them.*

PAR. *Yes,* SOCRATES, *said Parmenides; that is because you
are still young; the time will come, if I am not mistaken,
when philosophy will have a firmer grasp of you, and
then you will not despise even the meanest things; at
your age, you are too much disposed to regard the
opinions of men. But I should like to know whether
you mean that there are certain ideas of which all other
things partake, and from which they derive their names;
that similars, for example, become similar, because they
partake of similarity; and great things become great,
because they partake of greatness; and that just and
beautiful things become just and beautiful, because they
partake of justice and beauty?*

SOC. *Yes, certainly, said Socrates, that is my meaning.*

PAR. *Then each individual partakes either of the whole
of the idea or else of a part of the idea? Can there be
any other mode of participation?*

SOC. *There cannot be, he said.*

PAR. *Then do you think that the whole idea is one, and
yet, being one, is in each one of the many?*

SOC. *Why not,* PARMENIDES? *said Socrates.*

PAR. *Because one and the same thing will exist as a whole
at the same time in many separate individuals, and will
therefore be in a state of separation from itself.*

SOC. *Nay, but the idea may be like the day which is one
and the same in many places at once, and yet continu-
ous with itself; in this way each idea may be one and
the same in all at the same time.*

PAR. *I like your way,* SOCRATES, *of making one in many*

places at once. You mean to say, that if I were to spread out a sail and cover a number of men, there would be one whole including many—is not that your meaning?

SOC. *I think so.*

PAR. *And would you say that the whole sail includes each man, or a part of it only, and different parts different men?*

SOC. *The latter.*

PAR. *Then,* SOCRATES, *the ideas themselves will be divisible, and things which participate in them will have a part of them only and not the whole idea existing in each of them?*

SOC. *That seems to follow.*

PAR. *Then would you like to say,* SOCRATES, *that the one idea is really divisible and yet remains one?*

SOC. *Certainly not, he said.*

PAR. *Suppose that you divide absolute greatness, and that of the many great things, each one is great in virtue of a portion of greatness less than absolute greatness—is that conceivable?*

SOC. *No.*

PAR. *Or will each equal thing, if possessing some small portion of equality less than absolute equality, be equal to some other thing by virtue of that portion only?*

SOC. *Impossible.*

PAR. *Or suppose one of us to have a portion of smallness; this is but a part of the small, and therefore the absolutely small is greater; if the absolutely small be greater, that to which the part of the small is added will be smaller and not greater than before.*

SOC. *How absurd!*

PAR. *Then in what way,* SOCRATES, *will all things participate in the ideas, if they are unable to participate in them either as parts or wholes?*

SOC. *Indeed, he said, you have asked a question which is not easily answered.*

Metaphysics is that branch of philosophy which is concerned with investigating the nature of the truly and ultimately real.

Plato's metaphysics is based on his doctrine of forms, in which the incompatible views of two of his great pre-Socratic predecessors, Heraclitus and Parmenides, are integrated by a synthesis in which the opposed doctrines retain their truth but are no longer contradictory.

This was the sort of synthesis which Hegel, in the eighteenth century, later set up as the pattern for a new type of logic, or dialectic, which was Hegel's most distinctive contribution to philosophy.

For Heraclitus, the basic attribute of reality was change and impermanence; for Parmenides the basic attribute of reality was unchanging permanence.

Heraclitus, in a famous saying, observed that no one can step into the same river twice, because the water is continually flowing.

Heraclitus taught that the symbol of reality, and the basic substance out of which it is composed, is fire, which is ceaselessly changing. The description that Heraclitus offered of the nature of reality was vivid, pictorial, and applicable to the world which we know through our senses.

In the empirical world, that is, the world which we know through our senses, change is the ultimate principle to which every other principle must bow.

Not only do rivers move, but mountains crumble away, even if only a grain of dust at a time.

The world of modern physics is the world of ceaseless flux and change of Heraclitus. The permanence and rigidity and stability of such things as chairs and tables, in our every-day world, are discovered by the modern physicist to be wholly illusory. Physical objects are resolved into molecules, and atoms, and electrons which are perpetually in a state of change and flux.

Parmenides was one of the first great abstract thinkers in the history of the world. He was a rigorous logician, and he accepted the conclusions of his logic no matter how paradoxical and inconsistent with the reports of every-day common sense experience they might be. He was thus, first and last, a rationalist; for him the testimony of reason was supreme.

In attacking the problem as to the nature of ultimate reality, Parmenides began with the simple but fundamental logical principles which Aristotle was later to name the laws of Identity and Contradiction.

In Aristotle's terminology the law of identity can be stated as; whatever is, is. Or, in formal terms, "A is A."

The law of contradiction then, in its simplest expression, would be, whatever is not, is not, or as Aristotle later put it more precisely: "Nothing can both be and not be, at the same time, in the same place, and in the same sense." Stated formally, "A is not non-A."

These two basic laws of thought were used by Aristotle as the first premises of his system of logic, which has dominated philosophy to the present day; and while it has been supplemented, it has never been supplanted.

The word "being" is derived from the verb "to be," and thus designates an abstraction, the meaning of which is determined by the meaning of the verb "to be."

Instead of coining the word "being" from the infinitive form "to be," an exactly equivalent, but perhaps more readily intelligible term, "isness" can be constructed from one of the simpler forms of the verb, the third person singular present "is."

An abstract noun, derived from a verb which itself is the symbol for an action which we can perceive by our senses, is easily intelligible. The word "fighting" immediately suggests to the mind a specific case, such as "John fights Harry," from which we derive the content of the meaning of the term. The abstract noun form symbolized by "ing" furnishes the added meaning that the word "fighting" is intended to apply to any and all possible cases.

An abstract noun derived from a verb which is itself in turn abstract, as are all verbs, is about as bewildering and unintelligible a conception to the beginner in philosophy as he will ever encounter.

Unlike the former case, where the mind is able to grasp a specific content of a specific action, such as fighting, as the key to the meaning of the final abstraction, in the case of a word like "being," the key to the meaning of the final abstraction is itself an abstraction, and therefore, to most minds, quite baffling.

Severe mental discipline is required to understand the meaning of the word "being." We have found that the word "isness" is somewhat easier to grasp, apparently because the specific cases such as "A is B," "C is D," seem to have more content for the average mind than the completely abstract verb, "to be."

The central problem of philosophy for Parmenides, to which he devoted his whole life, was what is the meaning of the word "being," or, as we prefer to put it, "isness."

His starting point was the deceptively simple observation that "whatever is, is, and whatever is not, is not." Whatever is, is in the realm of "being" or "isness," whatever is not, is in the "void," which is completely blank, devoid of all "being," or "isness."

But if we grant this much, we are committed to the inescapable conclusion that change is impossible, because nothing can come out of the void, since there is nothing in the void.

For anything to change, it must become that which it is not, but things can either be, or not be. If anything gives up characters, these characters go into the void, a realm of non-being from which there is no returning. So Parmenides concluded that in the world of being, change is impossible.

Just as Heraclitus argued that permanence was an illusion, so Parmenides argued that change and motion were an illusion.

Zeno, the famous mathematician, was an enthusiastic disciple of Parmenides. He argued the case for his master by propounding several ingenious riddles and paradoxes which baffled mathematicians for thousands of years. His most famous paradox was the riddle of Achilles and the Tortoise. If Achilles gives the tortoise a head start in a race, he can never overtake him. Before Achilles can overtake the Tortoise, he must cover half the distance which separates them. While Achilles is traveling half the distance which separates him from the tortoise, the tortoise moves from point one to point two. Thus before Achilles can overtake the tortoise he must traverse half the distance which now separates him from point two, while he is doing so the tortoise moves to point three, and so on to infinity.

Plato's reconciliation of the views of Heraclitus and Parmenides consisted of accepting the description of Heraclitus as a faithful and literal report of the world which is known to us through our senses, the world of sights and sounds; and the report of Parmenides as the faithful and literal account of the world which we know through our minds, or the world of ideas.

Plato agreed with Parmenides that true reality was the world of being, unchanging and immutable, a unity; he also agreed with Heraclitus that the world in which we live is impermanent and transient and in a state of ceaseless flux. He concluded, therefore, that we do not live in the real world, the world of true being, but in an imitation world which only approximates the reality that only the world of the mind can discover.

Ideas are patterns or forms, which participate in the approximations of our every-day world. For example, the idea of circularity is the form or pattern constituting the ideal standard by means of which a rule for making approximations with drawing instruments is furnished.

While no circle drawn by the draftsman or geometer can ever be a real circle in the absolute sense, since to be drawn it must have breadth, the participation of the pure idea of circularity in the approximation called an empirical "circle" makes it possible for the world of ideas to rule the world of flux and impress on it a pattern or order akin to that of the world of ideas itself.

The "Parmenides" is obviously a Platonic, rather than Socratic, writing. Socrates is portrayed as a young man who has not mastered logic sufficiently well to be willing to follow out the implications of an argument when he discovers that the conclusions to which it leads are disagreeable to him.

We hardly need to point out that in subordinating the

personality of Socrates to that of Parmenides, Plato intended no slight upon his beloved master, but instead, by this device, he signs his name for posterity to the views presented in this dialogue.

The Search for Justice

SINCE THE SEARCH FOR JUSTICE in the individual has reached an impasse, Socrates proposes to turn to the state, where justice can be found with much greater ease. Since justice is the virtue of the State as well as of the individual, and since the state is so much larger than the individual, the story of justice is inscribed in the state in a much more legible fashion than it is written in the individual.

(From "The Republic")

SOCRATES *Glaucon and the rest entreated me by all means not to let the question drop, but to proceed in the investigation. They wanted to arrive at the truth, first, about the nature of justice and injustice, and secondly, about their relative advantages. I told them, what I really thought, that the inquiry would be of a serious nature, and would require very good eyes. Seeing then, I said, that we are no great wits, I think that we had better adopt a method which I may illustrate thus; suppose that a short-sighted person had been asked by some one to read small letters from a distance; and it occurred to some one else that they might be found in another place which was larger and in which the letters were larger—if they were the same and he could read the larger letters first, and then proceed to the lesser—this would have been thought a rare piece of good fortune.*

ADEIMANTUS *Very true, said Adeimantus; but how does the illustration apply to our inquiry?*

SOC. *I will tell you, I replied; justice, which is the subject of our inquiry, is, as you know, sometimes spoken of as the virtue of an individual, and sometimes as the virtue of a State.*

AD. *True, he replied.*

SOC. *And is not a State larger than an individual?*

AD. *It is.*

SOC. *Then in the larger the quantity of justice is likely to be larger and more easily discernible. I propose therefore that we inquire into the nature of justice and injustice, first as they appear in the State, and secondly in the individual, proceeding from the greater to the lesser and comparing them.*

SOC. *Then, I said, let us begin and create in idea a State; and yet the true creator is necessity, who is the mother of our invention.*

AD. *Of course, he replied.*

SOC. *Now the first and greatest of necessities is food, which is the condition of life and existence.*

AD. *Certainly.*

SOC. *The second is a dwelling, and the third clothing and the like.*

AD. *True.*

SOC. *And now let us see how our city will be able to supply this great demand: We may suppose that one man is a husbandman, another a builder, some one else a weaver—shall we add to them a shoemaker, or perhaps some other purveyor to our bodily wants?*

AD. *Quite right.*

SOC. *The barest notion of a State must include four or five men.*

AD. *Clearly.*

SOC. *And how will they proceed? Will each bring the result of his labors into a common stock? . . . or will he have nothing to do with others and not be at the trouble of producing for them, but provide for himself alone. . . .*

SOC. *And will you have a work better done when the workman has many occupations, or when he has only one?*

AD. *When he has only one.*

SOC. *And if so, we must infer that all things are produced more plentifully and easily and of a better quality*

*when one man does one thing which is natural to him
and does it at the right time, and leaves other things.*

AD. *Undoubtedly.*

SOC. *Then more than four citizens will be required; for
the husbandman will not make his own plough or mat-
tock, or other implements of agriculture, if they are to
be good for anything. Neither will the builder make his
tools—and he too needs many; and in like manner the
weaver and shoemaker.*

AD. *True.*

SOC. *Then carpenters, and smiths, and many other artisans, will be sharers in our little State, which is already
beginning to grow?*

AD. *True.*

SOC. *Yet even if we add neatherds, shepherds, and other
herdsmen, in order that our husbandmen may have oxen
to plough with, and builders as well as husbandmen may
have draught cattle, and curriers and weavers fleeces
and hides,—still our State will not be very large.*

AD. *That is true; yet neither will it be a very small State
which contains all these.*

SOC. *Then, again, there is the situation of the city—to
find a place where nothing need be imported is well-
nigh impossible.*

AD. *Impossible.*

SOC. *Then there must be another class of citizens who
will bring the required supply from another city?*

AD. *There must.*

SOC. *But if the trader goes empty-handed, having nothing
which they require who would supply his need, he will
come back empty-handed.*

AD. *That is certain.*

SOC. *And therefore what they produce at home must be
not only enough for themselves, but such both in quantity and quality as to accommodate those from whom
their wants are supplied.*

AD. *Very true.*

SOC. *Then more husbandmen and more artisans will be
required?*

AD. *They will.*

soc. *Not to mention the importers and exporters, who are called merchants?*

AD. *Yes.*

soc. *Then we shall want merchants?*

AD. *We shall.*

soc. *And if merchandise is to be carried over the sea, skillful sailors will also be needed, and in considerable numbers?*

AD. *Yes, in considerable numbers.*

soc. *Then, again, within the city, how will they exchange their productions? To secure such an exchange was, as you will remember, one of our principal objects when we formed them into a society and constituted a State.*

AD. *Clearly they will buy and sell.*

soc. *Then they will need a market-place, and a money-token for purposes of exchange.*

AD. *Certainly.*

soc. *Suppose now that a husbandman, or an artisan, brings some production to market, and he comes at a time when there is no one to exchange with him—is he to leave his calling and sit idle in the market-place?*

AD. *Not at all; he will find people there who, seeing the want, undertake the office of salesmen. In well-ordered states they are commonly those who are the weakest in bodily strength, and therefore of little use for any other purpose; their duty is to be in the market, and to give money in exchange for goods to those who desire to sell and to take money from those who desire to buy.*

soc. *This want, then, creates a class of retail-traders in our State. Is not 'retailer' the term which is applied to those who sit in the market-place engaged in buying and selling, while those who wander from one city to another are called merchants?*

AD. *Yes, he said.*

soc. *And there is another class of servants, who are intellectually hardly on the level of companionship; still they have plenty of bodily strength for labor, which accordingly they sell, and are called, if I do not mistake, hirelings, hire being the name which is given to the price of their labor.*

AD. *True.*

SOC. *Then hirelings will help to make up our population?*

AD. *Yes.*

SOC. *And now,* ADEIMANTUS, *is our State matured and perfected?*

AD. *I think so.*

SOC. *Where, then, is justice, and where is injustice, and in what part of the State did they spring up?*

AD. *Probably in the dealings of these citizens with one another.*

"The Republic" is the greatest masterpiece of social and political philosophy ever written. It has probably had more influence on human thought and the development of western civilization than any book, with the exception of the Bible. At the same time, it ranks as one of the four great masterpieces of Plato's literary and dramatic art, the other three being the "Phaedo," the "Protagoras" and the "Symposium."

In the "Republic," Socrates is essentially only a voice for Plato's own views, not only on social and political philosophy, but for the expression of the essence of Platonism, the doctrine of Forms. Ostensibly, the "Republic" is concerned with the discussion of the meaning and the possibility of the attainment of justice. In fact, it turns out to be a literary and dramatic tour-de-force by means of which Plato breathes life into his abstruse philosophical doctrines.

For instance, in the parable of the cave, we find the kind of literary skill which makes abstract ideas concrete, a capacity we will not again encounter in our study of the Great Ideas until we meet Schopenhauer.

In the first two books of the "Republic," Socrates attempts to defend the thesis that: it is better to be just than unjust. He is able to dispose of Thrasymachus, the blustering sophist who presents the view that might makes right, with his customary facility.

Glaucon and Adeimantus, brothers of Plato, even though both are diametrically opposed to the position of

Thrasymachus, feel that Socrates has not done justice to his own argument. Accordingly, in turn they present the case for the advantages of being unjust so overwhelmingly that Socrates for once is silenced, particularly by the parable of the ring of Gyges.

Instead of meeting the arguments directly, Socrates resorts instead to the trick with which our citation begins, namely, that of abandoning the search for justice in the individual, where the "letters are too small," and looking for it in the state, by reading the "larger letters first."

In searching for the definition of justice on the state level, Socrates examines the composition of the state itself, especially the division of labor. He shows how market-places and money grow out of specialization. Starting with one man, in order to make sure that justice does not slip through his fingers, Plato creates an imaginary state. Plato's exposition, which is a reduction to the lowest denominator, is both simple and plausible. From the very start it becomes apparent that "justice and injustice arise in some fashion in the dealings of the citizens of the state with one another."

Men of Gold, Silver and Iron

PLATO, LIKE JESUS, knew the value of the parable, and used it often. One of the most effective parables in the writings of Plato is the parable of the men of gold, the men of silver, and the men of brass and iron; the idea which it expresses has been confirmed by modern science and is now axiomatic in its world-wide acceptance.

(From "The Republic")

SOCRATES *Well then, I will speak, although I really know not how to look you in the face, or in what words to utter the audacious fiction, which I propose to communicate gradually, first to the rulers, then to the soldiers, and lastly to the people. They are to be told that their youth was a dream, and the education and training which they received from us, an appearance only; in reality during all that time they were being formed and fed in the womb of the earth, where they themselves and their arms and appurtenances were manufactured; when they were completed, the earth, their mother, sent them up; and so, their country being their mother and also their nurse, they are bound to advise for her good, and to defend her against attacks, and her citizens they are to regard as children of the earth and their own brothers.*

GLAUCON *You had good reason, he said, to be ashamed of the lie which you were going to tell.*

SOC. *True, I replied, but there is more coming; I have only told you half. Citizens, we shall say to them in our tale, you are brothers, yet God has framed you differently. Some of you have the power of command, and in the composition of these he has mingled gold, wherefore also they have the greatest honor; others he has*

*made of silver, to be auxiliaries; others again who are
to be husbandmen and craftsmen he has composed of
brass and iron; and the species will generally be preserved in the children. But as all are of the same original stock, a golden parent will sometimes have a silver
son, or a silver parent a golden son. And God proclaims
as a first principle to the rulers, and above all else, that
there is nothing which they should so anxiously guard,
or of which they are to be such good guardians, as of
the purity of the race. They should observe what
elements mingle in their offspring; for if the son of a
golden or silver parent has an admixture of brass and
iron, then nature orders a transposition of ranks, and
the eye of the ruler must not be pitiful towards the
child because he has to descend in the scale and become
a husbandman or artisan, just as there may be sons of
artisans who having an admixture of gold or silver in
them are raised to honor, and become guardians or
auxiliaries. For an oracle says that when a man of brass
or iron guards the State, it will be destroyed. Such is
the tale; is there any possibility of making our citizens
believe in it?*

GLAUC. *Not in the present generation, he replied; there is
no way of accomplishing this; but their sons may be
made to believe in the tale, and their sons' sons, and
posterity after them.*

A man should be judged for his own worth, for what
he can accomplish himself, and not because of his particular background. An individual with sufficient ability
should never be deprived of the opportunity to become
president of the United States just because he comes
from the other side of the tracks. But, on the other hand,
the son of a president need not necessarily be elected
president simply because of his birth.

Long before there were such things as vocational
guidance clinics, or even civil service, Plato saw the
need for such organizations.

Plato believed that if a person showed ability in a
particular direction, whether it be as a statesman or as

a saddle-maker, the opportunity for him to develop his ability should be provided. He believed that the state should set up schools which would be truly democratic in furnishing an equal chance to every child born in the state, and of realizing his potentialities to the fullest extent.

This, in essence, is the basis for the public school system in America.

But Plato would have extended this idea through trade schools, colleges, universities and professional schools.

In our present system, men and women are too often squeezed into jobs which they have inherited, jobs which they must do because their fathers and grandfathers before them did the same thing to earn a living. In Plato's system no such compulsions would exist.

If, for example, the son of a U. S. Senator showed no ability for politics or statesmanship, but demonstrated to his early teachers an aptitude for playing the harmonica, under a Platonic system the senator's son would become a happy musician instead of an incompetent and unhappy politician.

Plato had his own ideas about insuring honesty in government, a problem which has plagued us since the stone age. He would have forbidden anyone who served in the military or legislative branches of the government the right to own private property. But, on the other hand, he would have made those offices so attractive and filled with such honor, that the men who held them would become the most respected members of the state.

Furthermore, Plato would have screened out as ineligible for public service, everyone who could not put loyalty and patriotism and devotion to the pursuit of wisdom above every other consideration as the final purpose of his existence.

The ominous note of the oracle (as quoted in the text): "When a man of brass or iron guards the state . . . it will be destroyed," has been sounded many times in our culture. History offers numerous examples of the "iron man" who rose to "guard" the state. The oracle

has echoed and re-echoed down the corridors of civilization from Dionysius, the tyrant of Sicily, to Hitler, the
"iron man," and tyrant of the Third Reich, and the
prophecy of the oracle has always been made true.

How to Abolish Graft and Wars

PLATO HERE PROPOSES a plan that would take all material gain out of being a soldier or ruler. The plan is simple enough. Neither rulers nor warriors are to be permitted to have private property of their own. Every other group in the State, however, will continue to enjoy private property and free enterprise. Thus the rulers will not govern for the sake of acquiring personal fortunes, nor will the soldiers fight for loot. Instead, the state will be guarded and ruled by men of genuine patriotism and high mindedness. Graft will be abolished, and wars will be fought only for defense.

(From "The Republic")

SOCRATES *Yes, I said; but they must be the houses of soldiers, and not of shopkeepers.*
GLAUCON *What is the difference? he said.*
SOC. *That I will endeavor to explain, I replied. To keep watchdogs, who, from want of discipline or hunger, or some evil habit or other, would turn upon the sheep and worry them, and behave not like dogs but wolves, would be a foul and monstrous thing in a shepherd?*
GLAU. *Truly monstrous, he said.*
SOC. *And therefore every care must be taken that our auxiliaries, being stronger than our citizens, may not grow to be too much for them and become savage tyrants instead of friends and allies?*
GLAU. *Yes, great care should be taken.*
SOC. *And would not a really good education furnish the best safeguard?*
GLAU. *But they are well-educated already, he replied.*
SOC. *I cannot be so confident, my dear GLAUCON, I said; I am much more certain that they ought to be, and that*

true education, whatever that may be, will have the greatest tendency to civilize and humanize them in their relations to one another, and to those who are under their protection.

GLAU. *Very true, he replied.*

SOC. *And not only their education, but their habitations, and all that belongs to them, should be such as will neither impair their virtue as guardians, nor tempt them to prey upon the other citizens. Any man of sense must acknowledge that.*

GLAU. *He must.*

SOC. *Then now let us consider what will be their way of life, if they are to realize our idea of them. In the first place, none of them should have any property of his own beyond what is absolutely necessary; neither should they have a private house or store closed against any one who has a mind to enter; their provisions should be only such as are required by trained warriors, who are men of temperance and courage; they should agree to receive from the citizens a fixed rate of pay, enough to meet the expenses of the year and no more; and they will go to mess and live together like soldiers in a camp. Gold and silver we will tell them that they have from God; the diviner metal is within them, and they have therefore no need of the dross which is current among men, and ought not to pollute the divine by any such earthly admixture; for that commoner metal has been the source of many unholy deeds, but their own is undefiled. And they alone of all the citizens may not touch or handle silver or gold, or be under the same roof with them, or wear them, or drink from them. And this will be their salvation, and they will be the saviors of the State. But should they ever acquire homes or lands or moneys of their own, they will become housekeepers and husbandmen instead of guardians, enemies and tyrants instead of allies of the other citizens; hating and being hated, plotting and being plotted against, they will pass their whole life in much greater terror of internal than of external enemies, and the hour of ruin, both to themselves and to the rest of the State, will be at hand. For all which*

reasons may we not say that thus shall our State be ordered, and that these shall be the regulations appointed by us for our guardians concerning their houses and all other matters?
GLAU. *Yes, said Glaucon.*

The objection that is most frequently raised to Plato's Utopian schemes is that they do not sufficiently take human nature into account. And yet it is because he knows human nature so very well that Plato makes his most radical proposal. He had witnessed the exploitation of conquered peoples, by soldiers and rulers who were given the privilege of looting by their own people; and he had seen these same soldiers and rulers turn like wolves upon their very own people. As Plato so well puts it: "Since our soldiers are stronger than our citizens the state must insist that they behave like watchdogs and not like wolves."

Our own American state follows the recommendations of Plato more closely in respect to our soldiers than our rulers. We have tried to safeguard ourselves against too much control by the military. The Constitution itself guards the citizens against encroachments by soldiers, and the commander-in-chief of the entire military establishment is a civilian, the President. We have tried to take the profit out of war by income tax measures, and we have seen to it that the military man lives frugally and owns no property except that which is necessary. Nor is he permitted to keep any of the "loot" of war.

Among our rulers, we have many who approach the ideal set by Plato. Occasionally, however, we hear of a candidate for political office spending $100,000 on a campaign to win a $10,000 job. It is only too clear that particularly when the candidate is spending someone else's money, as is often the case, it is the public treasury that will have to pay it back.

It is an obvious misconception to accuse Plato of having been an advocate of "communism." He considered democracy to be the best of the realizable forms of government. He abhorred tyranny and dictatorship, and it was in order to safeguard against the state ever being taken over by a military or political dictatorship that he insisted upon the abolition of all private property for *soldiers and rulers* alone.

Justice As The Harmony of The Parts in a Whole

HERE PLATO makes the pronouncement that Justice does not demand happiness of the individual members of the state, but rather that each fulfill the functions for which he is best suited by his ability and education. The parable of the painted statue adds force and vividness.

(From "The Republic")

SOCRATES *Here Adeimantus interposed a question: How would you answer,* SOCRATES, *said he, if a person were to say that you are making these people miserable, and that they are the cause of their own unhappiness; the city in fact belongs to them, but they are none the better for it; whereas other men acquire lands, and build large and handsome houses, and have everything handsome about them, offering sacrifices to the gods on their own account, and practising hospitality; moreover, as you were saying just now, they have gold and silver, and all that is usual among the favorites of fortune; but our poor citizens are no better than mercenaries who are quartered in the city and are always mounting guard?*
SOC. *And our answer will be that, even as they are, our guardians may very likely be the happiest of men; but that our aim in founding the State was not the disproportionate happiness of any one class, but the greatest happiness of the whole; we thought that in a State which is ordered with a view to the good of the whole we should be most likely to find justice, and in the ill-ordered State injustice: and, having found them, we might then decide which of the two is the happier. At present, I take it, we are fashioning the happy State, not piecemeal, or with a view of making a few happy citizens, but as a whole; and by-and-by we will proceed to view the opposite kind of State. Suppose that we were painting a statue, and some one came up to us and said,*

Why do you not put the most beautiful colors on the most beautiful parts of the body—the eyes ought to be purple, but you have made them black—to him we might fairly answer, Sir, you would not surely have us beautify the eyes to such a degree that they are no longer eyes; consider rather whether, by giving this and the other features their due proportion, we make the whole beautiful. And so I say to you, do not compel us to assign to the guardians a sort of happiness which will make them anything but guardians; for we too can clothe ou·husbandmen in royal apparel, and set crowns of gold on their heads, and bid them till the ground as much as they like, and no more. Our potters also might be allowed to repose on couches, and feast by the fireside, passing round the winecup, while their wheel is conveniently at hand, and working at pottery only as much as they like; in this way we might make every class happy—and then, as you imagine, the whole State would be happy. But do not put this idea into our heads; for, if we listen to you, the husbandman will be no longer a husbandman, the potter will cease to be a potter, and no one will have the character of any distinct class in the State. Now this is not of much consequence where the corruption of society, and pretension to be what you are not, is confined to cobblers; but when the guardians of the laws and of the government are only seeming and not real guardians, then see how they turn the State upside down; and on the other hand they alone have the power of giving order and happiness to the State. We mean our guardians to be true saviors and not the destroyers of the State, whereas our opponent is thinking of peasants at a festival, who are enjoying a life of revelry, not of citizens who are doing their duty to the State. But, if so, we mean different things, and he is speaking of something which is not a State. And therefore we must consider whether in appointing our guardians we would look to their greatest happiness individually, or whether this principle of happiness does not rather reside in the State as a whole. But if the latter be the truth, then the guardians and auxiliaries, and all other equally with them, must be compelled or induced to do their own work in the best way. And thus the whole State will grow up in a noble order, and the several classes will receive the proportion of happiness which nature assigns to them.

Plato would not be willing to grant that the guardians of his state are not the happiest of all men. As a matter of fact, it is difficult to see how they could be anything but happy. By their hereditary endowment they have the ability and the temperament, and by their education they have the training, which makes them the kind of people for whom their work has become an end in itself, and its own reward. By being assured of the privilege of being permitted to engage in the very activities which they would choose first if they could do anything that they wanted, they are being guaranteed the greatest possible happiness.

Much the same could be said for the other classes in the state, with one important qualification. While the men of brass and iron, like the guardians, will be performing the functions in the state for which their native ability and training best suits them, unlike the guardians, they may become jealous of the men who hold positions with talents and abilities superior to their own, and may therefore be unhappy in jobs which they wrongly consider menial and beneath them.

The reply of Plato to the objection that he is not providing for the happiness of the individual members or classes of his state, while it may be adequate as pure theory, is fundamentally inadequate from a practical point of view.

Plato's rejoinder is that the concern of the state is not with the individual happiness of its individual members, but with the greatest happiness of the whole, the creation of a harmonious order in which the parts work together cooperatively, each doing the job for which it was designed, like the parts in a complex machine. The insurmountably practical objection to Plato's theory, at least at present, is that there are many jobs in a state which are important, but menial or mechanical and require so little training or ability for their execution, that, for the most part, those who remain in these occupations do so only because they are maintained in a sort of economic serfdom.

Take the men who dig our coal today. No one can deny that many of these men have remained coal miners, not because they didn't have the ability to take on a more intellectual or artistic job, or one requiring ability in commerce, technology or science, but rather because they never had the opportunity to be trained in anything but coal mining. And the same is true for numerous other occupations which are filled with men who, if they had had the proper chance, could have carried on a higher level job.

While we are building utopias it would not be difficult to imagine, as some science-fiction writers have done, a state in which technological advances have eliminated all menial and mechanical occupations, which have been turned over to robots, thereby making it possible for every man to realize himself to the limits of his potential. In such a state there would be no conflict between the happiness of the individual and the greatest happiness of the whole.

The Evils of Wealth and Poverty

PLATO INTRODUCES the utopian proposal that in the perfect state, there will be neither poverty nor monopolistic riches, and hints at the economic basis of the struggle between classes, which has since divided the world into two armed camps.

(From "The Republic")

SOCRATES *There seem to be two causes of the deterioration of the arts.*
ADEIMANTUS *What are they?*
SOC. *Wealth, I said, and poverty.*
AD. *How do they act?*
SOC. *The process is as follows: When a potter becomes rich, will he, think you, any longer take the same pains with his art?*
AD. *Certainly not.*
SOC. *He will grow more and more indolent and careless?*
AD. *Very true.*
SOC. *And the result will be that he becomes a worse potter?*
AD. *Yes; he greatly deteriorates.*
SOC. *But, on the other hand, if he has no money, and cannot provide himself with tools or instruments, he will not work equally well himself, nor will he teach his sons or apprentices to work equally well.*
AD. *Certainly not.*
SOC. *Then, under the influence either of poverty or of wealth, workmen and their work are equally liable to degenerate?*
AD. *That is evident.*
SOC. *Here, then, is a discovery of new evils, I said, against which the guardians will have to watch, or they will creep into the city unobserved.*

AD. *What evils?*

SOC. *Wealth,* I said, *and poverty; the one is the parent of luxury and indolence, and the other of meanness and viciousness, and both of discontent.*

AD. *That is very true, he replied; but still I should like to know,* SOCRATES, *how our city will be able to go to war, especially against an enemy who is rich and powerful, if deprived of the sinews of war.*

SOC. *There would certainly be a difficulty,* I replied, *in going to war with one such enemy; but there is no difficulty where there are two of them.*

AD. *How so? he asked.*

SOC. *In the first place,* I said, *if we have to fight, our side will be trained warriors fighting against an army of rich men.*

AD. *That is true, he said.*

SOC. *And do you not suppose,* ADEIMANTUS, *that a single boxer who was perfect in his art would easily be a match for two stout and well-to-do gentlemen who were not boxers?*

AD. *Hardly, if they came upon him at once.*

SOC. *Why, not,* I said, *if he were able to run away, and then turn and strike at the one who first came up? And supposing he were to do this several times under the heat of scorching sun, might he not, being an expert, overturn more than one stout personage?*

AD. *Certainly, he said, there would be nothing wonderful in that.*

SOC. *And yet rich men probably have a greater superiority in the science and practise of boxing than they have in military qualities.*

AD. *Likely enough.*

SOC. *Then we may assume that our athletes will be able to fight with two or three times their own number?*

AD. *I agree with you, for I think you right.*

SOC. *And suppose that, before engaging, our citizens send an embassy to one of the two cities, telling them what is the truth: Silver and gold we neither have nor are permitted to have, but you may; do you therefore come and help us in war, and take the spoils of the other city:*

Who, on hearing these words, would choose to fight against lean wiry dogs, rather than, with the dogs on their side, against fat and tender sheep?

AD. *That is not likely; and yet there might be a danger to the poor State if the wealth of many States were to be gathered into one.*

SOC. *But how simple of you to use the term State at all of any but our own!*

AD. *Why so?*

SOC. *You ought to speak of other States in the plural number; not one of them is a city, but many cities, as they say in the game. For indeed any city, however small, is in fact divided into two, one the city of the poor, the other of the rich; these are at war with one another; and in either there are many smaller divisions, and you would be altogether beside the mark if you treated them all as a single State. But if you deal with them as many, and give the wealth or power or persons of the one to the others, you will always have a great many friends and not many enemies. And your State, while the wise order which has now been prescribed continues to prevail in her, will be the greatest of States, I do not mean to say in reputation or appearance, but in deed and truth, though she number not more than a thousand defenders. A single State which is her equal you will hardly find, either among Hellenes or barbarians, though many that appear to be as great and many times greater.*

Plato's sophisticated analysis of wealth and poverty, as the causes of the deterioration of the arts, gains its plausibility from the fact that in the every-day world, there are artisans who are more concerned with their pay than with their art. Such men will, as Plato argues, become more indolent and careless with their work as they grow richer, provided they have become rich enough.

On the other hand, we might object to Plato's argument by pointing out, as he himself does, that the reverse may well hold, and an artist who is permitted to remain unduly poverty-stricken will also deteriorate. The necessity of earning his living may force him to produce "pot-boilers," whatever his field of art may be. Only when he is reasonably independent of economic pressures is he able to create genuine works of art.

It is apparent, however, that wealth is the condition and not the cause which results in an improvement or deterioration of the arts. The true artisan, like the true artist, finds his rewards not only in his pay, but in the craftsmanship, and in the artistic expression of his work itself.

Plato is perhaps being more realistic than we are when he warns us of the possibility that even in his Utopian republic, the artisans might not be completely indifferent to the charms of wealth.

If wealth is eliminated, then the arts will not be corruptible, according to Plato.

One of the chief difficulties of making a critical evaluation of "The Republic" is the shift that inevitably takes place in the application of arguments to a utopian world, and arguments applicable to the real, practical world in which we live. The danger of wealth may apply to the real world, but not the utopian world. People in the actual world have been conditioned to emphasize the importance of wealth. In Plato's utopian world, the factor of wealth would have far less weight, because while it is true that the artisans would be permitted to own private property, they too would have had enough philosophical training to prevent them from being conditioned in such a way as to overemphasize the importance of money.

The most important interpretation of Plato's teachings is perhaps found in their application to the problem of the state like our own, in which human nature has been conditioned by the actual experience we have had, rather than to a utopian state where human nature would be different, as a result of an entirely different set of conditioning processes.

In the actual world, excessive poverty and excessive

wealth are matters which have increasingly become the concern of the state, and even in the United States of today, both extreme poverty and excessive wealth are slowly being abolished by the federal government.

Equal Rights and Duties for Women

HERE PLATO is concerned with women's rights. It was to be more than 2,000 years before women were emancipated in the western world. Yet Plato has anticipated every sound argument of the modern feminist.

(From "The Republic")

SOCRATES *What I mean may be put into the form of a question, I said: Are dogs divided into hes and shes, or do they both share equally in hunting and in keeping watch and in the other duties of dogs? or do we entrust to the males the entire and exclusive care of the flocks, while we leave the females at home, under the idea that the bearing and suckling their puppies is labor enough for them?*

GLAUCON *No, he said, they share alike; the only difference between them is that the males are stronger and the females weaker.*

SOC. *But can you use different animals for the same purpose, unless they are bred and fed in the same way?*

GLAU. *You cannot.*

SOC. *Then, if women are to have the same duties as men, they must have the same nurture and education?*

GLAU. *Yes.*

SOC. *The education which was assigned to the men was music and gymnastic.*

GLAU. *Yes.*

SOC. *Then women must be taught music and gymnastic and also the art of war, which they must practise like the men?*

GLAU. *That is the inference, I suppose.*

SOC. *I should rather expect, I said, that several of our proposals, if they are carried out, being unusual, may appear ridiculous.*

GLAU. *No doubt of it.*

soc. Yes, and the most ridiculous thing of all will be the sight of women naked in the palaestra, exercising with the men, especially when they are no longer young; they certainly will not be a vision of beauty, any more than the enthusiastic old men who in spite of wrinkles and ugliness continue to frequent the gymnasia.

soc. First, then, whether the question is to be put in jest or in earnest, let us come to an understanding about the nature of woman: Is she capable of sharing either wholly or partially in the actions of men, or not at all? And is the art of war one of those arts in which she can or can not share? That will be the best way of commencing the inquiry, and will probably lead to the fairest conclusion.

soc. Then let us put a speech into the mouths of our opponents. They will say: 'Socrates and Glaucon, no adversary need convict you, for you yourselves, at the first foundation of the State, admitted the principle that everybody was to do the one work suited to his own nature.' And certainly, if I am not mistaken, such an admission was made by us. 'And do not the natures of men and women differ very much indeed?' And we shall reply: Of course they do. Then we shall be asked, 'Whether the tasks assigned to men and to women should not be different, and such as are agreeable to their different natures?' Certainly they should. 'But if so, have you not fallen into a serious inconsistency in saying that men and women, whose natures are so entirely different, ought to perform the same actions?'—What defense will you make for us, my good Sir, against any one who offers these objections?

soc. Well then, let us see if any way of escape can be found. We acknowledged—did we not? that different natures ought to have different pursuits, and that men's and women's natures are different. And now what are we saying?—that different natures ought to have the same pursuits,—this is the inconsistency which is charged upon us.

GLAU. *Precisely.*

SOC. *Verily,* GLAUCON, *I said, glorious is the power of the art of contradiction!*

GLAU. *Why do you say so?*

SOC. *Because I think that many a man falls into the practice against his will. When he thinks that he is reasoning he is really disputing, just because he cannot define and divide, and so know that of which he is speaking; and he will pursue a merely verbal opposition in the spirit of contention and not of fair discussion.*

SOC. *Suppose that by way of illustration we were to ask the question whether there is not an opposition in nature between bald men and hairy men; and if this is admitted by us, then, if bald men are cobblers, we should forbid the hairy men to be cobblers, and conversely?*

GLAU. *That would be a jest, he said.*

SOC. *Yes, I said, a jest; and why? because we never meant when we constructed the State, that the opposition of natures should extend to every difference, but only to those differences which affected the pursuit in which the individual is engaged; we should have argued, for example, that a physician and one who is in mind a physician may be said to have the same nature.*

GLAU. *True.*

SOC. *Whereas the physician and the carpenter have different natures?*

GLAU. *Very true, he said.*

SOC. *And if, I said, the male and female sex appear to differ in their fitness for any art or pursuit, we should say that such pursuit or art ought to be assigned to one or the other of them; but if the difference consists only in women bearing and men begetting children, this does not amount to a proof that a woman differs from a man in respect of the sort of education she should receive; and we shall therefore continue to maintain that our guardians and their wives ought to have the same pursuits.*

GLAU. *Very true, he said.*

SOC. *Come now, and we will ask you a question:—when you spoke of a nature gifted or not gifted in any respect, did you mean to say that one man will acquire a thing easily, another with difficulty; a little learning will lead the one to discover a great deal; whereas the other, after much study and application, no sooner learns than he forgets; or again, did you mean, that the one has a body which is a good servant to his mind, while the body of the other is a hindrance to him?—would not these be the sort of differences which distinguish the man gifted by nature from the one who is ungifted?*

GLAU. *No one will deny that.*

SOC. *And can you mention any pursuit of mankind in which the male sex has not all these gifts and qualities in a higher degree than the female?*

SOC. *And if so, my friend, I said, there is no special faculty of administration in a state which a woman has because she is a woman, or which a man has by virtue of his sex, but the gifts of nature are alike diffused in both; all the pursuits of men are the pursuits of women also, but in all of them a woman is inferior to a man.*

GLAU. *Very true.*

SOC. *Then are we to impose all our enactments on men and none of them on women?*

GLAU. *That will never do.*

SOC. *One woman has a gift of healing, another not; one is a musician, and another has no music in her nature?*

GLAU. *Very true.*

SOC. *And one woman has a turn for gymnastic and military exercises, and another is unwarlike and hates gymnastics?*

GLAU. *Certainly.*

SOC. *And one woman is a philosopher, and another is an enemy of philosophy; one has spirit, and another is without spirit?*

GLAU. *This is also true.*

SOC. *Then one woman will have the temper of a guardian, and another not. Was not the selection of the male guardians determined by differences of this sort?*

GLAU. *Yes.*

SOC. *Men and women alike possess the qualities which*

make a guardian; they differ only in their comparative strength or weakness.

GLAU. *Obviously.*

SOC. *And those women who have such qualities are to be selected as the companions and colleagues of men who have similar qualities and whom they resemble in capacity and in character?*

GLAU. *Very true.*

SOC. *And ought not the same natures to have the same pursuits?*

GLAU. *They ought.*

SOC. *Then, as we were saying before, there is nothing unnatural in assigning music and gymnastic to the wives of the guardians—to that point we come round again.*

GLAU. *Certainly not.*

SOC. *The law which we then enacted was agreeable to nature, and therefore not an impossibility or mere aspiration; and the contrary practice, which prevails at present, is in reality a violation of nature.*

SOC. *Then let the wives of our guardians strip, for their virtue will be their robe, and let them share in the toils of war and the defence of their country; only in the distribution of labors the lighter are to be assigned to the women, who are the weaker natures, but in other respects their duties are to be the same. And as for the man who laughs at naked women exercising their bodies from the best of motives, in his laughter he is plucking 'A fruit of unripe wisdom,' and he himself is ignorant of what he is laughing at, or what he is about—for that is, and ever will be, the best of sayings, That the useful is the noble and the hurtful is the base.*

Here is a citation for those who wonder whether a woman will ever be able to become president of the United States.

Writing at a time when women were considered almost an intermediate species between man and animal, and except in rare cases, had a fate hardly superior to that of servants, Plato's views are all the more remarkable.

It is true that Plato did not hold that women were fully the equal of men in all respects. What Plato argued was that:

(a) Women are inferior in muscular strength, which for the most part we can grant. Although in exceptional cases even this may not be true.

(b) Women are endowed with the same talents and potentialities in all fields of human endeavor that men are, but also always to a less degree. That is women, like men, are divided into those of gold, of silver, and of brass or iron. Any woman of gold or silver is superior to any man of brass or iron. But there will always be a man of gold who is the superior of any woman of gold, and so on through each of the ranks.

This typically masculine prejudice of Plato seems to have been borne out so far by history, but since the number of women who have been privileged to compete with men in their own fields has been exceedingly small, the number of women who have distinguished themselves is remarkably large, considering the total numbers of men and women who are represented in these competitions.

The liberality of Plato's views is a direct consequence of his rigorous application of one of the cardinal principles of "The Republic," the principle that each person in the state must perform the function for which he is best fitted.

And rare as they may have been, the fact that some women like Sappho had demonstrated to the world that they were made of gold, made it imperative that in Plato's state no woman of talent should be relegated to a life of merely cooking and baking and housekeeping.

Plato must have been well aware that his revolutionary views on the emancipation of women would be derided and ridiculed. This did not deter him from championing their case, and in the famous epigram "let our women strip and their virtue be their robe,"* Plato effectively silenced any unfair attacks.

---

* Compare the motto of the Order of the Knights of the Garter: "Honi soit qui mal y pense." (Evil to him who evil thinks.)

In our times the views of Plato have become so commonplace that we have seen women in the Congress, as governors, on the benches of Federal courts, in the Senate and even in the Cabinet of the President. No woman has ever been on the bench of the Supreme Court or ever held the office of vice-president. For a woman to achieve any of the goals not yet reached will require a combination of talents far beyond those required had she been a man. It would be a rash person who would predict that this could never happen. Yet if the day should come when the resident of the White House would be addressed as Madame President, this would be more than Plato himself could have envisioned.

Was Plato Practical?

THE CREATOR of a Utopia pauses to consider the prac-
ticality of his schemes, and offers a proposal to make his
Utopia practicable, which many consider to be his most
Utopian scheme of all.

(From "The Republic")

SOCRATES *Let me begin by reminding you that we
found our way hither in the search after justice and
injustice.*
GLAUCON *True, he replied; but what of that?*
SOC. *I was only going to ask whether, if we have discovered them, we are to require that the just man should
in nothing fail of absolute justice; or may we be satisfied
with an approximation, and the attainment in him of a
higher degree of justice than is to be found in other men?*
GLAU. *The approximation will be enough.*
SOC. *We were inquiring into the nature of absolute justice
and into the character of the perfectly just, and into injustice and the perfectly unjust, that we might have an
ideal. We were to look at these in order that we might
judge of our own happiness and unhappiness according to
the standard which they exhibited and the degree in
which we resembled them, but not with any view of
showing that they could exist in fact.*
GLAU. *True, he said.*
SOC. *Would a painter be any the worse because, after
having delineated with consummate art an ideal of a
perfectly beautiful man, he was unable to show that any
such man could ever have existed?*
GLAU. *He would be none the worse.*
SOC. *Well, and were we not creating an ideal of a perfect
State?*

GLAU. *To be sure.*

SOC. *And is our theory a worse theory because we are unable to prove the possibility of a city being ordered in the manner described?*

GLAU. *Surely not, he replied.*

SOC. *That is the truth, I said. But if, at your request, I am to try and show how and under what conditions the possibility is highest, I must ask you, having this in view, to repeat your former admissions.*

GLAU. *What admissions?*

SOC. *I want to know whether ideals are ever fully realized in language? Does not the word express more than the fact, and must not the actual, whatever a man may think, always, in the nature of things, fall short of the truth? What do you say?*

GLAU. *I agree.*

SOC. *Then you must not insist on my proving that the actual State will in every respect coincide with the ideal: if we are only able to discover how a city may be governed nearly as we proposed, you will admit that we have discovered the possibility which you demand; and will be contented. I am sure that I should be contented— will not you?*

GLAU. *Yes, I will.*

SOC. *Let me next endeavor to show what is that fault in States which is the cause of their present maladministration, and what is the least change which will enable a State to pass into the truer form; and let the change, if possible, be of one thing only, or, if not, of two; at any rate, let the changes be as few and slight as possible.*

GLAU. *Certainly, he replied.*

SOC. *I think, I said, that there might be a reform of the State if only one change were made, which is not a slight or easy though still a possible one.*

GLAU. *What is it? he said.*

SOC. *Now then, I said, I go to meet that which I liken to the greatest of the waves; yet shall the word be spoken, even though the wave break and drown me in laughter and dishonor; and do you mark my words.*

GLAU. *Proceed.*

soc. *I said:* Until philosophers are kings, or the kings and princes of this world have the spirit and power of philosophy, and political greatness and wisdom meet in one, and those commoner natures who pursue either to the exclusion of the other are compelled to stand aside, cities will never have rest from their evils,—no, nor the human race, as I believe,—and then only will this our State have a possibility of life and behold the light of day. *Such was the thought, my dear* GLAUCON, *which I would fain have uttered if it had not seemed too extravagant; for to be convinced that in no other State can there be happiness private or public is indeed a hard thing.*

GLAU. SOCRATES, *what do you mean? I would have you consider that the word which you have uttered is one at which numerous persons, and very respectable persons too, in a figure pulling off their coats all in a moment, and seizing any weapon that comes to hand, will run at you might and main, before you know where you are. . . .*

Perhaps the most devastating criticism that any political reformer must face is the challenge: "Yes, it looks good on paper, but will it work?"

Plato had no delusions about the applicability of his program for the reform of a world like our own. Anticipating the inevitable objections that his plans for a "republic" are impractical, he counters by agreeing that they are, and always will be, in any government ruled by politicians. Only in a state where philosophers are kings could his plan ever be realized. In a famous passage, which is quoted in the citation above, and which will bear repeating, Plato states that:

> Until philosophers are kings, or the kings and princes
> of this world have the spirit and power of philosophy,
> and political greatness and wisdom meet in one, and those
> commoner natures who pursue either to the exclusion
> of the other are compelled to stand aside, cities will never
> have rest from their evils,—no, nor the human race, as
> I believe,—and then only will this our State have a
> possibility of life and behold the light of day.

From his own point of view, Plato's argument is final and unanswerable. But has he met the challenge of practicability?

The problem of the practicability of the Republic is not with the second generation of citizens in the Republic. They will have been conditioned so effectively, that it will be unthinkable to them to elect any one but the philosophers as their rulers. But it is the first generation, which has not been so conditioned, that faces a permanent stalemate in Plato's game of chess.

Plato was as aware of this factor as any of his critics have ever been, and perhaps even better than most of them. After all, he had the unique experience which he relates in his autobiographical "Seventh Epistle," of having served for a year as personal advisor on affairs of state to Dionysius, the young tyrant of Sicily, who unfortunately was not a philosopher. Thus at least the negative implications of Plato's great paradox, namely, that a philosopher cannot reform a state by merely serving as an advisor, or brain trust, as long as the ruler is a politician, had been demonstrated to him in his own experience.

Whether the philosopher would be any more successful even if he were to take over the actual rule of an existing state is probably just as unlikely. The second generation in the state would accept him as the Hitler youth accepted Hitler, but the first generation of non-philosophers would no more give up their old ideals and convictions, than the fathers of the Hitler youth, who fought against their own sons in the underground against the Nazi regime, were willing to give up their own inborn convictions.

The fatal flaw in the practicability of a Platonic republic is that we need the first generation to produce and bring up the second. But we could never have a state in which every parent would indoctrinate his own children with a culture antithetical to his own.

When Philosophers Are Kings

ADEIMANTUS objects that for philosophers to be kings, is the most wild-eyed impractical idealism of all. Plato re-convinces his readers by having Socrates relate the parable of the pilot and the ship of state.

(From "The Republic")

ADEIMANTUS   *Here Adeimantus interposed and said: To these statements, Socrates, no one can offer a reply; but when you talk in this way, a strange feeling passes over the minds of your hearers: They fancy that they are led astray a little at each step in the argument, owing to their own want of skill in asking and answering questions; these littles accumulate, and at the end of the discussion they are found to have sustained a mighty overthrow and all their former notions appear to be turned upside down. And as unskillful players of draughts are at last shut up by their more skillful adversaries and have no piece to move, so they too find themselves shut up at last; for they have nothing to say in this new game of which words are the counters; and yet all the time they are in the right. The observation is suggested to me by what is now occurring. For any one of us might say, that although in words he is not able to meet you at each step of the argument, he sees as a fact that the votaries of philosophy, when they carry on the study, not only in youth as a part of education, but as pursuit of their maturer years, most of them become strange monsters, not to say utter rogues, and that those who may be considered the best of them are made useless to the world by the very study which you extol.*

SOCRATES   *Well, and do you think that those who say so are wrong?*

AD. *I cannot tell, he replied; but I should like to know what is your opinion.*

SOC. *Hear my answer; I am of opinion that they are quite right.*

AD. *Then how can you be justified in saying that cities will not cease from evil until philosophers rule in them, when philosophers are acknowledged by us to be of no use to them?*

SOC. *You ask a question, I said, to which a reply can only be given in a parable.*

AD. *Yes,* SOCRATES; *and that is a way of speaking to which you are not at all accustomed, I suppose.*

SOC. *I perceive, I said, that you are vastly amused at having plunged me into such a hopeless discussion; but now hear the parable, and then you will be still more amused at the meagreness of my imagination: for the manner in which the best men are treated in their own States is so grievous that no single thing on earth is comparable to it; and therefore, if I am to plead their cause, I must have recourse to fiction, and put together a figure made up of many things, like the fabulous unions of goats and stags which are found in pictures. Imagine then a fleet or a ship in which there is a captain who is taller and stronger than any of the crew, but he is a little deaf and has a similar infirmity in sight, and his knowledge of navigation is not much better. The sailors are quarreling with one another about the steering—every one is of opinion that he has a right to steer, though he has never learned the art of navigation and cannot tell who taught him or when he learned, and will further assert that it cannot be taught, and they are ready to cut in pieces any one who says the contrary. They throng about the captain, begging and praying him to commit the helm to them; and if at any time they do not prevail, but others are preferred to them, they kill the others or throw them overboard, and having first chained up the noble captain's senses with drink or some narcotic drug, they mutiny and take possession of the ship and make free with the stores; thus, eating and drinking, they proceed on their voyage in such a manner as might be expected of them. Him who*

*is their partisan and cleverly aids them in their plot for
getting the ship out of the captain's hands into their own
whether by force or persuasion, they compliment with
the name of sailor, pilot, able seaman, and abuse the
other sort of man, whom they call a good-for-nothing;
but that the true pilot must pay attention to the year
and seasons and sky and stars and winds, and whatever
else belongs to his art, if he intends to be really qualified
for the command of a ship, and that he must and will be
the steerer, whether other people like or not—the possibility of this union of authority with the steerer's art has
never seriously entered into their thoughts or been made
part of their calling. Now in vessels which are in a state
of mutiny and by sailors who are mutineers, how will the
true pilot be regarded? Will he not be called by them a
prater, a star-gazer, a good-for-nothing?*

AD. *Of course, said Adeimantus.*

SOC. *Then you will hardly need, I said, to hear the interpretation of the figure, which describes the true philosopher in his relation to the State; for you understand
already.*

AD. *Certainly.*

SOC. *Then suppose you now take this parable to the
gentleman who is surprised at finding that philosophers
have no honor in their cities; explain it to him and try to
convince him that their having honor would be far more
extraordinary.*

AD. *I will.*

SOC. *Say to him, that, in deeming the best votaries of
philosophy to be useless to the rest of the world, he is
right; but also tell him to attribute their uselessness to the
fault of those who will not use them, and not to themselves. The pilot should not humbly beg the sailors to be
commanded by him—that is not the order of nature;
neither are 'the wise to go to the doors of the rich'— the
ingenious author of this saying told a lie—but the truth
is, that, when a man is ill, whether he be rich or poor, to
the physician he must go, and he who wants to be governed, to him who is able to govern. The ruler who
is good for anything ought not to beg his subjects to be*

*ruled by him; although the present governors of mankind
are of a different stamp; they may be justly compared to
the mutinous sailors, and the true helmsmen to those who
are called by them good-for-nothings and star-gazers.*

Adeimantus complains about Socrates' method of argument. He says that the teacher convinces his opponent
piecemeal, step by step in the discussion, forcing one
admission after another, so that when the final conclusion
is reached the opponent not only does not like it but he
does not even remember how it was arrived at. All this
will bring a sympathetic smile to the face of the reader
who has had the same treatment at the hands of Socrates.

The initial plausibility of Plato's figure of the pilot and
his crew wears off a bit when we stop to wonder whether
the state is really like a ship, and whether a ruler is really
like a navigator.

No one can deny that on a ship, the pilot should be the
man skilled in navigation, rather than the men who have
the physical strength to seize the tiller from the captain's
hand regardless of whether they know anything about
navigation or not.

Does the analogy hold, however? A navigator who sets
out to steer a ship from one port to another has a map,
with a clearly defined course on it, and all he has to do is
to make some rather simple observations and solve some
rather simple mathematical problems (for which, inci-
dentally, he has formulas) in order to reach his goal.

Insofar as the captain of a ship is more than a navigator, he may need some of the very qualities such as
strength, leadership, and the respect of his men, and the
ability to deal justly with them, which would make it
unlikely that his ship would ever be taken from him.
But we can let that pass, because as we enlarge on the
requirements for being a good captain, we are beginning
to develop the requirements for being the ruler of the
crew, rather than the navigator of the ship; and it is just
this difference which needs to be sharpened in order to
appreciate the inapplicability of Plato's analogy. In the
first place, a ruler is an administrator, and there are no

charts and maps and formulas which he can use for charting his own course. It is true that there are certain statistical rules which he can apply in influencing large groups of people, such as the various occupational politically-factional groups in his state. But his real test is met in his dealings with individuals, and here there are no rules to guide him but his own intuitive grasp of the good, and his ability as a leader.

The Parable of The Cave

THE PINNACLE of Plato's philosophy is his doctrine of Forms, the great idea with which his name will always be identified as long as men live. It is here presented in a parable which is the greatest masterpiece of literary art in the history of secular philosophy.

(From "The Republic")

SOCRATES *And now, I said, let me show in a figure how far our nature is enlightened or unenlightened:— Behold! human beings living in an underground den, which has a mouth open towards the light and reaching all along the den; here they have been from their childhood, and have their legs and necks chained so that they cannot move, and can only see before them, being prevented by the chains from turning round their heads. Above and behind them a fire is blazing at a distance, and between the fire and the prisoners there is a raised way; and you will see, if you look, a low wall built along the way, like the screen which marionette players have in front of them, over which they show the puppets.*

GLAUCON *I see.*

SOC. *And do you see, I said, men passing along the wall carrying all sorts of vessels, and statues and figures of animals made of wood and stone and various materials, which appear over the wall? Some of them are talking, others silent.*

GLAU. *You have shown me a strange image, and they are strange prisoners.*

SOC. *Like ourselves, I replied; and they see only their own shadows, or the shadows of one another, which the fire throws on the opposite wall of the cave?*

GLAU. *True, he said; how could they see anything but the shadows if they were never allowed to move their heads?*

soc. *And of the objects which are being carried in like manner they would only see the shadows?*

GLAU. *Yes, he said.*

soc. *And if they were able to converse with one another, would they not suppose that they were naming what was actually before them?*

GLAU. *Very true.*

soc. *And suppose further that the prison had an echo which came from the other side, would they not be sure to fancy when one of the passers-by spoke that the voice which they heard came from the passing shadow?*

GLAU. *No question, he replied.*

soc. *To them, I said, the truth would be literally nothing but the shadows of the images.*

GLAU. *That is certain.*

soc. *And now look again, and see what will naturally follow if the prisoners are released and disabused of their error. At first, when any of them is liberated and compelled suddenly to stand up and turn his neck round and walk and look towards the light, he will suffer sharp pains; the glare will distress him, and he will be unable to see the realities of which in his former state he had seen the shadows; and then conceive some one saying to him, that what he saw before was an illusion, but that now, when he is approaching nearer to being and his eye is turned towards more real existence, he has a clearer vision,—what will be his reply? And you may further imagine that his instructor is pointing to the objects as they pass and requiring him to name them,—will he not be perplexed? Will he not fancy that the shadows which he formerly saw are truer than the objects which are now shown to him?*

GLAU. *Far truer.*

soc. *And if he is compelled to look straight at the light, will he not have a pain in his eyes which will make him turn away to take refuge in the objects of vision which he can see, and which he will conceive to be in reality clearer than the things which are now being shown to him?*

GLAU. *True, he said.*

SOC. *And suppose once more, that he is reluctantly dragged up a steep and rugged ascent, and held fast until he is forced into the presence of the sun himself, is he not likely to be pained and irritated? When he approaches the light his eyes will be dazzled, and he will not be able to see anything at all of what are now called realities.*

GLAU. *Not all in a moment, he said.*

SOC. *He will require to grow accustomed to the sight of the upper world. And first he will see the shadows best, next the reflections of men and other objects in the water, and then the objects themselves; then he will gaze upon the light of the moon and the stars and the spangled heaven; and he will see the sky and the stars by night better than the sun or the light of the sun by day?*

GLAU. *Certainly.*

SOC. *Last of all he will be able to see the sun, and not mere reflections of him in the water, but he will see him in his own proper place, and not in another; and he will contemplate him as he is.*

GLAU. *Certainly.*

SOC. *He will then proceed to argue that this is he who gives the season and the years, and is the guardian of all that is in the visible world, and in a certain way the cause of all things which he and his fellows have been accustomed to behold?*

GLAU. *Clearly, he said, he would first see the sun and then reason about him.*

SOC. *And when he remembered his old habitation, and the wisdom of the den and his fellow-prisoners, do you not suppose that he would felicitate himself on the change, and pity them?*

GLAU. *Certainly, he would.*

SOC. *And if they were in the habit of conferring honors among themselves on those who were quickest to observe the passing shadows and to remark which of them went before, and which followed after, and which were together; and who were therefore best able to draw con-*

clusions as to the future, do you think that he would care for such honors and glories, or envy the possessors of them? Would he not say with Homer,

'Better to be the poor servant of a poor master,'
and to endure anything, rather than think as they do and live after their manner?

GLAU. *Yes, he said, I think that he would rather suffer anything than entertain these false notions and live in this miserable manner.*

SOC. *Imagine once more, I said, such an one coming suddenly out of the sun to be replaced in his old situation; would he not be certain to have his eyes full of darkness?*

GLAU. *To be sure, he said.*

SOC. *And if there were a contest, and he had to compete in measuring the shadows with the prisoners who had never moved out of the den, while his sight was still weak, and before his eyes had become steady (and the time which would be needed to acquire this new habit of sight might be very considerable), would he not be ridiculous? Men would say of him that up he went and down he came without his eyes; and that it was better not even to think of ascending; and if any one tried to loose another and lead him up to the light, let them only catch the offender, and they would put him to death.*

GLAU. *No question, he said.*

SOC. *This entire allegory, I said, you may now append, dear* GLAUCON, *to the previous argument; the prison-house is the world of sight, the light of the fire is the sun, and you will not misapprehend me if you interpret the journey upwards to be the ascent of the soul into the intellectual world according to my poor belief, which, at your desire, I have expressed—whether rightly or wrongly God knows. But, whether true or false, my opinion is that in the world of knowledge the idea of good appears last of all, and is seen only with an effort; and, when seen, is also inferred to be the universal author of all things beautiful and right, parent of light and the lord of light in this visible world, and the immediate source of reason and truth in the intellectual;*

*and that this is the power upon which he who would
act rationally either in public or private life must have
his eye fixed.*

GLAU. *I agree, he said, as far as I am able to understand
you.*

SOC. *Moreover, I said, you must not wonder that those
who attain to this beatific vision are unwilling to descend
to human affairs; for their souls are ever hastening into
the upper world where they desire to dwell; which desire of theirs is very natural, if our allegory may be
trusted.*

GLAU. *Yes, very natural.*

SOC. *And is there anything surprising in one who passes
from divine contemplations to the evil state of man,
misbehaving himself in a ridiculous manner; if, while his
eyes are blinking and before he has become accustomed
to the surrounding darkness, he is compelled to fight in
courts of law, or in other places, about the images or
the shadows of images of justice, and is endeavoring to
meet the conceptions of those who have never yet seen
absolute justice?*

GLAU. *Anything but surprising, he replied.*

It was Plato who said that philosophy is music in its
highest form.

In the figure of the cave, as in the speech of Diotima
in "The Symposium," Plato reaches heights that have
rarely been reached by any other composer, musical or
literary.

There is a double symbolism in the figure which like
the overture in an opera announces the principal themes
of the entire work. The principal theme of the figure
is the representation of Plato's heaven as the dwelling
place of God who is the light of reason symbolized by
the sun, and the eternal ideas or forms, or essences,
symbolized by the shadows they cast into the cave
which in turn represents the imperfect unreal world
of appearances and approximations in which we live
in bonds which fetter us to our bodies.

The subordinate theme symbolizes the argument of

"The Republic." We see the prisoner who is reluctantly dragged up the steep and rugged ascent to where he is forced to see the light of the sun itself. The prisoner represents the philosopher, whose long and rigorous training in philosophy and dialectic has culminated in his intuition of the idea of the good, and who is so dazzled by this vision that when he re-enters the cave he gropes about helplessly. He is unable to orient himself to a world of shadows and appearances instead of the world of realities into which he had climbed on the ladder of philosophical dialectic until he has readjusted himself to the darkness of the cave.

In the formal argument of "The Republic," Plato states that the future guardians will complete their philosophical studies at the age of forty. He then allows ten additional years for them to readjust their eyes to the cave. This readjustment consists of active participation in practical affairs.

The superior ability in the measurement of shadows which the prisoner who has seen the sun exhibits after his eyes have readjusted themselves to the darkness symbolizes Plato's immortal paradox: That "until philosophers are kings, or the kings and princes of this world have the spirit and power of philosophy, and political greatness and wisdom meet in one. . . ." only then can his Republic be realized.

Love Is of The Everlasting Possession
of The Good

THE SYMPOSIUM is unmistakably the work of the mature Plato at his best. The subordination of the character of Socrates to that of Diotima, the wise woman of Mantineia, serves as a subtle and artistic literary device by means of which Plato absolves Socrates of the responsibility for Plato's own views.

"The Symposium" has been acclaimed as Plato's literary masterpiece. It is indispensible for understanding Plato's most important philosophical doctrine, the doctrine of Forms. To understand philosophy, which is the love of wisdom, we must first understand what is meant by love. Let Diotima be our mentor.

(From "The Symposium")

SOCRATES *And now, taking my leave of you, I will rehearse a tale of love which I heard from Diotima of Mantineia, a woman wise in this and in many other kinds of knowledge . . . First I said to her in nearly the same words which he used to me, that Love was a mighty god, and likewise fair; and she proved to me as I proved to him that, by my own showing, Love was neither fair nor good. 'What do you mean, Diotima,' I said, 'is love then evil and foul?' 'Hush,' she cried; 'must that be foul which is not fair?' 'Certainly,' I said. 'And is that which is not wise, ignorant? do you not see that there is a mean between wisdom and ignorance?' 'And what may that be?' I said. 'Right opinion,' she replied; 'which, as you know, being incapable of giving a reason, is not knowledge (for how can knowledge be devoid of reason? nor again, ignorance, for neither can ignorance attain the truth), but is clearly something which is a mean between ignorance and wisdom.' 'Quite true,' I replied.*

'Do not then insist,' she said, 'that what is not fair is of necessity foul, or what is not good evil; or infer that because Love is not fair and good he is therefore foul and evil; for he is a mean between them.

'The truth of the matter is this: No god is a philosopher or seeker after wisdom, for he is wise already; nor does any man who is wise seek after wisdom. Neither do the ignorant seek after wisdom. For herein is the evil of ignorance, that he who is neither good nor wise is nevertheless satisfied with himself: he has no desire for that of which he feels no want.' 'But who then, Diotima,' I said, 'are the lovers of wisdom, if they are neither the wise nor the foolish?' 'A child may answer that question,' she replied; 'they are those who are in a mean between the two; Love is one of them. For wisdom is a most beautiful thing, and Love is of the beautiful; and therefore Love is also a philosopher or lover of wisdom, and being a lover of wisdom is in a mean between the wise and the ignorant. And of this too his birth is the cause; for his father is wealthy and wise, and his mother poor and foolish. Such, my dear Socrates, is the nature of the spirit of Love.'

I said: 'O thou stranger woman, thou sayest well; but, assuming Love to be such as you say, what is the use of him to men?' 'That, Socrates,' she replied, 'I will attempt to unfold: of his nature and birth I have already spoken; and you acknowledge that love is of the beautiful. But some one will say: Of the beautiful in what, Socrates and Diotima?—or rather let me put the question more clearly, and ask: When a man loves the beautiful, what does he desire?' I answered her 'That the beautiful may be his.' 'Still,' she said, 'the answer suggests a further question: What is given by the possession of beauty?' 'To what you have asked,' I replied, 'I have no answer ready.' 'Then,' she said, 'let me put the word "good" in the place of the beautiful, and repeat the question once more: If he who loves loves the good, what is it then that he loves?' 'The possession of the good,' I said. 'And what does he gain who possesses the good?' 'Happiness,' I replied; 'there is less difficulty in answering that question.'

'Yes,' she said, 'the happy are made happy by the acquisition of good things. Nor is there any need to ask
why a man desires happiness; the answer is already final.'
'You are right,' I said. 'And is this wish and this desire
common to all? and do all men always desire their own
good, or only some men?—what say you?' 'All men,' I
replied; 'the desire is common to all.' 'Why, then,' she
rejoined, 'are not all men, Socrates, said to love, but only
some of them? whereas you say that all men are always
loving the same things.' 'I myself wonder,' I said, 'why
this is.' 'There is nothing to wonder at,' she replied; 'the
reason is that one part of love is separated off and receives the name of the whole, but the other parts have
other names.' 'Give an illustration,' I said. She answered
me as follows: 'There is poetry, which, as you know, is
complex and manifold. All creation or passage of non-
being into being is poetry or making, and the processes
of all art are creative; and the masters of arts are all
poets or makers.' 'Very true.' 'Still,' she said, 'you know
that they are not called poets, but have other names;
only that portion of the art which is separated off from
the rest, and is concerned with music and metre, is
termed poetry, and they who possess poetry in this sense
of the word are called poets.' 'Very true,' I said. 'And
the same holds of love. For you may say generally that
all desire of good and happiness is only the great and
subtle power of love; but they who are drawn towards
him by any other path, whether the path of money-
making or gymnastics or philosophy, are not called lovers
—the name of the whole is appropriated to those whose
affection takes one form only—they alone are said to
love, or to be lovers.' 'I dare say,' I replied, 'that you
are right.' 'Yes,' she added, 'and you hear people say
that lovers are seeking neither for the half of themselves,
nor for the whole, unless the half or the whole be also
a good. And they will cut off their own hands and feet
and cast them away, if they are evil; for they love not
what is their own, unless perchance there be some one
who calls what belongs to him the good, and what belongs to another the evil. For there is nothing which men

*love but the good. Is there anything?' 'Certainly, I should
say, that there is nothing.' 'Then,' she said, 'the simple
truth is, that men love the good.' 'Yes,' I said. 'To which
must be added that they love the possession of the
good?' 'Yes, that must be added.' 'And not only the
possession, but the everlasting possession of the good?'*

*'That must be added too.' 'Then love,' she said, 'may
be described generally as the love of the everlasting
possession of the good?' 'That is most true.'*

*'Then if this be the nature of love, can you tell me
further,' she said, 'what is the manner of the pursuit?
what are they doing who show all this eagerness and
heat which is called love? and what is the object which
they have in view? Answer me.' 'Nay, Diotima,' I replied, 'if I had known, I should not have wondered at
your wisdom, neither should I have come to learn from
you about this very matter.' 'Well,' she said, 'I will teach
you:—The object which they have in view is birth of
beauty, whether of body or soul.' 'I do not understand
you,' I said; 'the oracle requires an explanation.' 'I will
make my meaning clearer,' she replied. 'I mean to say,
that all men are bringing to the birth in their bodies
and in their souls. There is a certain age at which human
nature is desirous of procreation—procreation which must
be in beauty and not in deformity; and this procreation
is the union of man and woman, and is a divine thing;
for conception and generation are an immortal principle
in the mortal creature, and in the inharmonious they
can never be. But the deformed is always inharmonious
with the divine, and the beautiful harmonious. Beauty,
then, is the destiny or goddess of parturition who pre-
sides at birth, and therefore, when approaching beauty,
the conceiving power is propitious, and diffusive, and
benign, and begets and bears fruit: at the sight of ugliness she frowns and contracts and has a sense of pain,
and turns away, and shrivels up, and not without a pang
refrains from conception. And this is the reason why,
when the hour of conception arrives, and the teeming
nature is full, there is such a flutter and ecstacy about*

beauty whose approach is the alleviation of the pain of travail. For love, Socrates, is not, as you imagine, the love of the beautiful only.' 'What then?' 'The love of generation and of birth in beauty.' 'Yes,' I said. 'Yes, indeed,' she replied. 'But why of generation?' 'Because to the mortal creature, generation is a sort of eternity and immortality,' she replied; 'and if, as has been already admitted, love is of the everlasting possession of the good, all men will necessarily desire immortality together with good: Wherefore love is of immortality.'

In the commentary on the figure of the cave, we spoke of music that was played as philosophy. If we were forced to make the difficult choice of selecting Plato's finest composition, we would award the palm to the aria in "The Symposium," the speech of Diotima. This is a hymn in praise of love itself.

A great aria can be best appreciated in its own context, and inevitably suffers when it is torn away from it. Modern gestalt psychologists have explained why a string of pearls gains in lustre and brilliance when it is placed on black velvet, the background and the context being vital factors in the total perception.

"The Symposium" as a supreme work of art has unity, balance, and dramatic contrast. The universality of its appeal through the centuries may be due in part to the fact that even those who are insensitive to philosophy can recognize its greatness.

The speech of Diotima is the climax of a carefully staged final curtain speech of a brilliantly-staged play. The play begins in a convivial and jolly mood at a banquet to celebrate a prize won by the poet Agathon, and after the guests have dined they decide to be entertained by conversation in the form of round-robin speeches. Love is suggested as the topic, and the first speeches made by Phaedrus, Pausanias and Eryximachus do little more than set the mood for the amazing half-serious speech of Aristophanes, the famous comic dramatist. Here Plato outdoes the real Aristophanes in a style not only worthy of Aristophanes himself, but which surpasses him at his own game.

No ordinary mortal would dare to speak after Aristophanes. That would be anti-climax. It took Socrates to surpass Aristophanes. After Socrates begins to speak what had gone before becomes trivial in significance.

Plato, through the device of having Socrates report the tale he heard from Diotima, is able to sound again the dominant themes which composed the Platonic philosophy.

The topic of love, which has been set for the discussion, is swept up in a flight of fancy which absorbs it, without a pause, in its flight into the profounder topic of the love of wisdom. The lover discussed by all preceding speakers thus is recognized as the philosopher.

The object of any lover is re-examined, and Plato discovers that what the lover loves, is the beauty of his beloved, which, as Plato has long taught, is at one with the good.

Under the spell of Plato, we rediscover in an old truth, implications we had never dreamed of. What the lover wants of the object of his love is to possess it, to possess its beauty, which is its goodness, and its truth. Thus he will achieve happiness, which is the possession of the good. Nor is the lover content to possess the good for a mere brief moment. He wants to possess the good, the beautiful, and the true, forever; and that is why he desires immortality.

Thus the familiar fact that the beautiful arouses the desire on the part of the beholder to possess it physically, is absorbed, and generalized, and sublimated in Plato's exposition. The love of the beautiful is the love of creation, of generation, of procreation—it is the love of birth in beauty, whether of body or of mind.

In his quest for the beautiful, the philosopher is midway between the ignorant and the wise. He is guided by "right opinion," which is the attainable compromise between ignorance and that true wisdom which only the gods can achieve. Through "right opinion," the philosopher learns to know and appreciate beauty, and truth and goodness, by starting with particular cases and approaching his goal as he nears the universal. His is the love, which is the love of wisdom, which is philosophy.

The True, The Good, and The Beautiful

DIOTIMA leads us to the good, the true, and the beautiful, which are one, by a discourse on the nature of beauty which has probably charmed more readers into becoming disciples of Plato than any other passage in the *Dialogues*.

(From "The Symposium")

DIOTIMA *'These are the lesser mysteries of love, into which even you,* SOCRATES, *may enter; to the greater and more hidden ones which are the crown of these, and to which, if you pursue them in a right spirit, they will lead, I know not whether you will be able to attain. But I will do my utmost to inform you, and do you follow if you can. For he who would proceed aright in this matter should begin in youth to visit beautiful forms; and first, if he be guided by his instructor aright, to love one such form only—out of that he should create fair thoughts; and soon he will of himself perceive that the beauty of one form is akin to the beauty of another; and then if beauty of form in general is his pursuit, how foolish would he be not to recognize that the beauty in every form is one and the same! And when he perceives this he will abate his violent love of the one, which he will despise and deem a small thing, and will become a lover of all beautiful forms; in the next stage he will consider that the beauty of the mind is more honorable than the beauty of the outward form. So that if a virtuous soul have but a little comeliness, he will be content to love and tend him, and will search out and bring to the birth thoughts which may improve the young, until he is compelled to contemplate and see the beauty of institutions and laws, and to understand that the beauty of them all is of one family, and that personal beauty is a trifle; and after laws and institutions he will go on to the sciences, that he may see their beauty, being not like a servant in love with the beauty of one youth or man or institution, himself a slave mean and narrow-minded, but drawing towards and contemplating the vast sea of beauty, he will create many fair and noble thoughts and notions in boundless love of wisdom; until on that shore he grows and waxes strong, and at last the vision is revealed to him of a single science, which is the science of beauty everywhere. To this I will proceed; please to give me your very best attention:*

He who has been instructed thus far in the things of love, and who has learned to see the beautiful in due order and succession, when he comes toward the end will suddenly perceive a nature of wondrous beauty (and this, SOCRATES, is the final cause of all our former toils)—a nature which in the first place is everlasting, not growing and decaying, or waxing and waning; secondly, not fair in one point of view and foul in another, or at one time or in one relation or at one place fair, at another time or in another relation or at another place foul, as if fair to some and foul to others, or in the likeness of a face or hands or any other part of the bodily frame, or in any form of speech or knowledge, or existing in any other being, as for example, in an animal, or in heaven, or in earth, or in any other place; but beauty absolute, separate, simple, and everlasting, which without diminution and without increase, or any change, is imparted to the ever-growing and perishing beauties of all other things. He who from these ascending under the influence of true love, begins to perceive that beauty, is not far from the end. And the true order of going, or being led by another, to the things of love, is to begin from the beauties of earth and mount upwards for the sake of that other beauty, using these as steps only, and from one going on to two, and from two to all fair forms, and from fair forms to fair practices, and from fair practices to fair notions, until from fair notions he arrives at the notion of absolute beauty, and at last knows what the essence of beauty is. This, my dear SOCRATES,' said the stranger of

Mantineia, 'is that life above all others which man should live, in the contemplation of beauty absolute; a beauty which if you once beheld, you would see not to be after the measure of gold, and garments, and fair boys and youths, whose presence now entrances you; and you and many a one would be content to live seeing them only and conversing with them without meat or drink, if that were possible—you only want to look at them and to be with them. But what if man had eyes to see the true beauty—the divine beauty, I mean, pure and clear and unalloyed, not clogged with the pollutions of mortality and all the colors and vanities of human life— thither looking, and holding converse with the true beauty simple and divine? Remember how in that communion only, beholding beauty with the eye of the mind, he will be enabled to bring forth, not images of beauty, but realities (for he has hold not of an image but of a reality), and bringing forth and nourishing true virtue to become the friend of God and be immortal, if mortal man may. Would that be an ignoble life?'

SOCRATES   *Such, PHAEDRUS—and I speak not only to you, but to all of you—were the words of Diotima; and I am persuaded of their truth. And being persuaded of them, I try to persuade others, that in the attainment of this end human nature will not easily find a helper better than love. And therefore, also, I say that every man ought to honor him as I myself honor him, and walk in his ways, and exhort others to do the same, and praise the power and spirit of love according to the measure of my ability now and ever.*

Aesthetics is that division of philosophy whose central concern is the meaning of beauty. No one has ever written a more significant treatise on aesthetics than that found in "The Symposium."

The moving principle of the whole history of art, from the first crude realistic representations of particular objects drawn by the cave man, to the expression of the most universal abstractions of modern art, is captured and expressed in "The Symposium."

The modern French impressionists like Cézanne, and abstractionists like Mondrian, are true disciples of Plato. Cézanne said that when he drew an apple he did not draw an apple, but appleness, that is, all apples. What he endeavored to capture and express is not the specific content which individualizes a particular apple. Rather he is seeking for the expression of the universal form or pattern, or idea, in the Platonic sense, which is not this apple, nor that apple, but every apple. When Picasso renders a figure in full face, in profile, from the outside, and from the inside, all at once, he is trying to express the essence, the innermost being, the pure form, the pure idea, just as Socrates outlines the long and rigorous training which is required before the soul is able to gain the power to recognize the highest form of beauty—universal beauty.

The pure form, or idea of beauty is devoid of all particular content. In the same way, long and arduous training in the principles of aethetics is required before we can go on from our ability to appreciate particular things, and pretty pictures of particular things, which are so realistically portrayed that we can see them as particulars, to the universal, which can only be suggested.

It is not enough for a picture of a tree to look like a particular tree—in so far as it is a successful work of art it must suggest all trees. The same principle holds in music, where we discover the superior beauty of particular sounds, as produced by particular instruments, but which express a mood, which in turn expresses an idea.

In this way, we discover in our study of aesthetics, that in our search for beauty we approach closer and closer as we leave the context of the particular form, and reach areas of greater and greater generality and universality. The quality of beauty present in a particular aesthetic object becomes more and more beautiful as we approach the unattainable ideal limit of the pure form or idea, totally devoid of empirical content, which is absolute beauty.

Epilogue

BELOVED PAN, and all ye other gods who know this place, give me beauty in the inward soul; and may the outward and inward man be at one. May I reckon the wise to be the wealthy and may I have such a quantity of gold as none but the temperate can carry. Anything more? That prayer, I think, is enough for me.

—SOCRATES